TEACH YOUR CHILDREN WELL

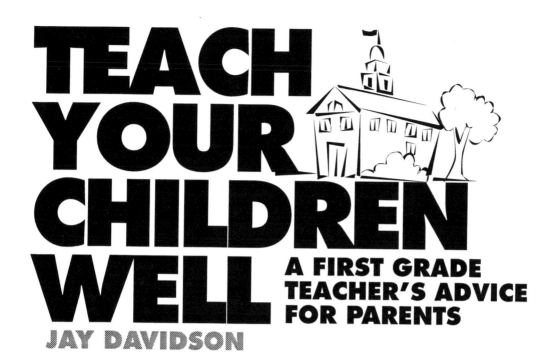

A FIRST GRADE TEACHER'S ADVICE FOR PARENTS

JAY DAVIDSON

D1476787

Also by Jay Davidson

BOOKLETS

65 Ideas for Reducing Stress

99 Ways to Guide Your Child to Success in School

301 Tips for Socially Responsible Travelers

WORKBOOK

My First Writing Dictionary

COLUMN

Teacher Talk

TEACH YOUR CHILDREN WELL

A FIRST GRADE TEACHER'S ADVICE FOR PARENTS

JAY DAVIDSON

TEACH YOUR CHILDREN WELL
A FIRST GRADE TEACHER'S ADVICE FOR PARENTS

Tojabrel Press

P. O. Box 51996

Palo Alto, CA 94303

Library of Congress Card Catalog Number: 00-191543

ISBN 0-9701273-0-8 (alk. paper)

Cover design and book design by Terri Hill, Designer Hill

Graphic Illustrations by Karen Soleau

Cover photo by Ben Janken Photography, Oakland, CA

Find the author on the Internet: www.jaydavidson.com

This book is dedicated to two vital groups of people:

TO PARENTS

You are your children's first and
most important teachers.
You have the most difficult, and (if you do it right)
the most time-consuming job that exists.
Nobody said it was going to be easy.
I have the utmost respect for you.

TO TEACHERS

My colleagues, you put untold hours
into the education of our youth.
Your dedication to your students is exemplary.
You have a passion that deserves
to be recognized.
We know you are not doing it for the pay,
the stock options, or the glory.

In memory of my former student
Hiram Kenneth Petitt
February 14, 1992 – July 30, 2000

ACKNOWLEDGMENTS

Just as the education of our young people is a cooperative process, so was the creation of this book. I am grateful for the wisdom and encouragement of many people:

My fellow teachers: Phyllis Matsuno, principal of Alvarado School, and Alvarado colleagues Aiko Cuneo, Joyce Romano, Laurie Baker-Flynn, Maggie Leigh, Paula Conrey, and Rosemary Hiller; Anne McGuire, Jim Mathiott, Marge Collins, Susan Sanford, and Suzanne Jones.

Alma Flor Ada and F. Isabel Campoy whose Teachers as Authors program kept a fire going.

My Advocate Circle members who hear from me at least once a month and offer their encouragement: Amanda Kovattana, Andrew Gross, Barbara Waugh, Beth Blair, Harold Lustig, Jennifer Rousseau Sedlock, Judi Kortz, Karla Jones, Kit Davey, Larry Dodd, Linda Howell, Marci Strange, Mark LeBlanc, Mary Dabaghian, Patti Breitman, Patti Glick, and Susan Hannah.

The National Association of Professional Organizers and especially the members of my chapter, San Francisco Bay Area, several of whom are in my Advocate Circle. Mary E. Rossow has helped with some insightful coaching.

Katy Obringer, Supervisor of Children's Library, and Maya Spector, Senior Librarian, Palo Alto City Library.

Monica DeHart de Galicia, Ph.D. candidate, Department of Cultural and Social Anthropology, and Dr. Shirley Brice Heath, English Department, Stanford University.

The enthusiastic and supportive membership of Lee Emerson Bassett Toastmasters.

Dave Price, my editor at the *Palo Alto Daily News*, who took a chance and began running my *Teacher Talk* column in 1998.

My own teachers who inspired me to enter this noble and rewarding profession: Mrs. Starrin, P. S. 64, Bronx, New York; Ted Savalas and Steve Darienzo, Lee Avenue School, and Jack Klein, Hicksville Junior High School, Hicksville, New York; Judith Rudman, Edda Perfetto, Irving Mulde, Adeline Davis, and Walter Matthews, West Hempstead High School, West Hempstead, New York; Allan Schramm, Roberta Barrett, and Lee Bryant, SUNY College at Oneonta; Mary Lane and Loretta Belgum, San Francisco State University; and Frances Reynolds, my master teacher at Cooperstown Central School, Cooperstown, New York.

My family - Tom, Brian, and Elizabeth, for whom I give thanks every day.

CONTENTS

PART 1: SKILLS

PART 2: VALUES

INTRODUCTION

As a public school teacher, I am pleased when parents have faith in my ability to educate their children. Is it feasible, however, for parents to expect that teachers alone will do this tremendous job?

Parents: you are your child's first, most important, and most consistent teacher. When the school year is completed each day and for the summer, the classroom teacher's work is done temporarily, but yours continues.

The three sections below give you insight for the premise of this book. I hope that the information will encourage you to maximize your participation in your child's education.

1. Let's do some math together

What percentage of your child's waking hours does she spend in school? Let's analyze the time a typical first-grader spends in direct classroom instruction. You may be surprised. Your child's hours may vary, depending on where he goes to school and how much he sleeps.

The school year in California has 180 days.

Each school day	360 minutes (6 hours)
Lunch	50 minutes
Recess	20 minutes
Transitions	30 minutes

(entering class in the morning, going to and coming from lunch and recess, dismissal)

Our six hours (360 minutes) of school has now been decreased to 260 minutes.

Multiply that by 180 school days and you get 46,800 minutes, or 780 hours per year.

Total hours per year 8,760 hours

Subtract hours spent sleeping 3,467.5 hours
(average of 9.5 hours per night)

Remaining hours per year 5,292.5 hours

The 780 hours of school are 14.73% of your child's waking hours during a year. Let's round that off to 15%.

Did you think that your child spent more than 15% of her waking hours in school? If her teacher(s) are responsible only for that small portion of time, who is taking care of the other 85%? This is you — the parents!

If a store were advertising that it was having a sale, with 15% off its usual prices, would you be impressed by the savings? Probably not, because you know how small 15% really is.

2. Encourage lifelong learning

What skills will your child need in order to be successful in life after school? Futurists try to anticipate what the world will be like by the time today's children enter the workforce. Take a backward look to your own aspirations when you were in elementary school. What did you want to be when you grew up?

Did your current job exist when you were a child? Look at some job titles on business cards I have in front of me: senior systems analyst, worldwide change manager, bureau chief, director of product management, humor consultant,membership account executive, principal player, group benefits specialist, and facilitator/support coordinator. How did the people in these jobs train for them if the jobs didn't exist when they were children? My point is this: we can't teach the specific skills that will be necessary because we do not know the jobs of the future. But we can teach our children the joy, wonder, and adventure that comes from learning — that there are fascinating and wonderful things to discover and to know. We can encourage the development of curiosity. We can show, by our own example, what it is like always to be willing and eager to learn and try something new. Furthermore, we can demonstrate that if we make a mistake, we can learn from it and move forward with a positive attitude to our next challenge. If we teach our children to be flexible, to be curious about learning new things, to solve problems, and to be willing to make mistakes while they are doing so, then we are teaching them how to prepare for their future.

3. Funding for education

How many rolls of wrapping paper, boxes of chocolate, and magazine subscriptions have you purchased or sold, fundraising for your child's school? How many silent auctions, book sales, bake sales, and rummage sales have you attended or helped to organize? Your participation in these events sends a strong message to your children that you are an active supporter of your school and your child's education, which is a good thing.

The media pays a lot of attention to each state's per-pupil spending. States are compared and ranked. Parents in states with higher spending are deceiving themselves into a false sense of security if they think that they, therefore, don't have anything to worry about. Parents in states with lower spending may feel that they can't do anything to improve their children's education.

There is something that no amount of fundraising, grant-writing, or taxes can pay for. That is the time that parents spend with their children. The only kind of *spending* that counts is the amount of time that parents *spend* with their children!

PART 1: SKILLS

Education is not a preparation for life; education is life itself.

— John Dewey

CHAPTER 1:
ORAL LANGUAGE

TALK, TALK, TALK

The four-year-old was excited as he saw something that caught his eye outside the bus. I was sitting behind him and his mother.

"Look, mama. It's a 'e'!" he said proudly, pointing to the letter he had learned to recognize, possibly in pre-school.

His mother's response stunned me: "Shut up!"

The little guy didn't say another word during the half hour that I continued sitting behind them.

Mom had missed one of the fundamental building blocks of learning: talking. It is through talking with children that we teach them ways to process their thinking, an understanding of the way our language works, and, above all, vocabulary. Frank Smith, a language researcher, tells us that children know an average of 20,000 words when they start kindergarten. Their way of learning these is through conversation.

Being able to speak and listen to oral language is a precursor to expressing oneself in writing, as well as being able to read the words that others have written.

I see the results of this in my classroom daily. There are some kids who can express, for example, where it was that they went to visit their relatives or what they did with their families, and others whose response is simply a shrug of their shoulders.

This is an ability that can easily be taught to children, if parents take the time to do it. "We're going to Uncle John and Aunt Elaine's house. They live in Sunnyvale. I'll bet you can remember that name; it's like the glorious sunny day we are having today."

Who is conversing with your children if you are not? In school, with twenty children in primary grade classrooms, your child speaks with peers, but there is not the same opportunity as they have with their parents for complex conversations with adults. Incessant chattering can be annoying to parents, but you need to see it as a necessary learning tool.

We should not be speaking to, but with. That is second nature to any good teacher.

— Noam Chomsky

After all, parents reap a generous benefit when they consciously work with their children to express themselves verbally. It is those same parents who ask questions for which they will want expressive and meaningful answers:

"What did you do in school today?"

"Nothing."

GET THE KIDS TALKING

These two books give parents a practical and constructive approach with regard to developing and maintaining conversations with their children:

How to Talk So Kids Will Listen & Listen So Kids Will Talk, by Adele Faber and Elaine Mazlish

How to Talk So Kids Can Learn: At Home and in School, by Adele Faber and Elaine Mazlish

PHONEMIC AWARENESS

A phrase that you may have heard your child's teacher use is *phonemic awareness*. It sounds a little like a word you probably know — *phonics* — and they are related because they both have to do with sounds.

Phonics refers to the relationship between letters and their sounds that are used in writing and reading. The premise of phonics is that every letter (or, in some cases, combinations of letters) has its own sound (and in some cases, they have more than one sound).

On the other hand, *phonemic awareness* refers to the ability to hear and tell the difference between words, sounds, and syllables in speech. These are four elements of phonemic awareness:

Rhyme

The goal is for children to recognize rhyme when they hear it and be able to produce rhymes on their own. Poems and songs are excellent for teaching rhymes. If you know the song "Down by the Bay," for example, this is an excellent way to teach this skill.

> *Down by the bay, where the watermelons grow,*
> *Back to my home, I dare not go,*
> *For if I do, my mother will say,*
> *"Have you ever seen a goat*
> *Sitting in a boat*
> *Down by the bay?"*

There is no limit to the possibilities, all of which need rhyming words: Have you ever seen a *whale* with a polkadot *tail*; Have you ever seen *Daniel* with a cocker *spaniel*, etc.

Hearing syllables

Children frequently begin to understand the concept of syllables when they clap them out for their own names. They can identify how many syllables are in words they or you say, and they can come up with words that have the number of syllables you ask for: two, three, four, etc.

Blending

This is an important concept because many words in our language have consonants that blend into each other. On the simplest level, we say or read the letters of words, like the sounds of *c*, *a*, and *t*. Then the child repeats them in order, first slowly, and then more quickly, until she is saying *cat*. In the reverse process, this is what we usually mean when we suggest that children "sound out" an unfamiliar word to see what it says.

Segmentation

When a child is writing a word, saying it slowly can help with the spelling. If the child asks, "How do you spell *sister*?" we help, not by giving the letters but by asking the child to give us the sounds that he hears. "What sound do you hear first? Then what sound?" We continue with the child, sound by sound, until there is a group of letters that represents the words. Even when words are not spelled correctly, this process helps with the learning of the sound-to-letter relationship.

PLAYING WITH WORDS

Rubber baby buggy bumpers. Peter Piper picked a peck of pickled peppers. Tongue twisters are a way to enjoy word play with your child. This helps to encourage the appreciation of words and language. It also develops listening skills.

A natural place to begin with younger children is to choose a letter or sound and find words that begin with the same letter or sound: *ball, bus, baby, bottle, bicycle*, etc. Once they get a handle on beginning sounds, move to ending sounds or middle sounds.

Let's look at a list of rhyming words: *an, ban, can, Dan, fan, Jan, man, Nan, pan, ran, Stan, tan, van*. Some are words that your child already knows. If he doesn't know some of them, this creates a teaching opportunity for you to explain the meaning of a new word.

If he offers responses such as *zan, gan,* or *han* you explain that yes, these are sounds that rhyme (always look for a way to give encouragement), but these aren't words.

There's no telling where you will go when you are teaching your child. Be open to the direction in which your conversation may lead.

"What about *san*?" she asks.

"Ah," you explain, "That's just like the San in San Francisco; it's a Spanish word that means saint. San Francisco was named after Saint Francis. There are other cities that start with San: San Diego, San Carlos, San Mateo. And Santa means saint for women: Santa Monica, Santa Clara, Santa Fe." Your word-play started with sounds and it led you to geography and Spanish!

This type of play is also easily transported to a variety of settings: the car, dinner table, grocery store, and park bench. It needs no equipment; all you need to carry with you is your own imagination.

Many families have children of different ages involved in the same conversation. If your younger child is approaching school age and is ready for this type of word play, remind the older one(s) of the importance of being non-judgmental in working with the little one(s). Enlist their aid in teaching what they know to their younger siblings. This will help to reinforce their own skills and abilities.

FOCUS ON POETRY

April is National Poetry Month. But it is not the only month when poetry is fun and instructive.

Kids in their early years of learning language are adventuresome in many ways. One of these is their exploration and use of language. You can help support that adventure.

Consider the popularity of nursery rhymes. They use rhythms and rhymes in a joyful and playful manner. The situations are silly. They connect kids to a common American culture. Many recall simpler times and activities: kids fetching a pail of water, a lamb following a girl to school, a boy jumping over a candlestick.

These sing-song rhythms help children develop an appreciation of the spoken language. Then, as children begin to read, they notice that there are spelling patterns. You can help your child to see that if they can spell one word and remember the pattern, they can then use this pattern to spell many other rhyming words.

These poems are often wonderful vocabulary builders, as children come into contact with words or phrases formerly unfamiliar to them. This gives you an opportunity to explain these concepts.

Many songwriters nowadays take the easy way out, trying to pass off such pairs as *came* and *sane* as rhymes. It's difficult to get kids to understand that these are not rhymes, if that is what they are used to hearing. You can help by setting a higher standard in the books you read with your child. Where do you begin?

WHO'S YOUR FAVORITE POET?

My students have many favorites. It's hard to beat the humor and inventiveness of Jack Prelutsky, who has several books on the market. He has all the features kids enjoy in poetry: silliness, great rhymes, and many surprises in the last lines of his poems.

Shel Silverstein was also prolific, with a sense of humor skewed toward slightly older kids.

There's no better writer to start with than Dr. Seuss, whose books are available everywhere.

The folks in the children's department at your favorite bookstore or library are in a good position to fill you in on their favorites.

EXPANDING YOUR CHILD'S VOCABULARY

On the last day of school, one of my students brought me a gift. She said, "I have a flower for you," and I realized that she didn't know what kind of flower it was. I responded by saying, "Thank you for the beautiful carnation."

This got me to thinking about nomenclature, and how common it is for children to understand general categories of words, but not necessarily specific ones within each category.

Parents can pay attention to the vocabulary that they use in conversation with their young ones. In helping children with more specific words, they can guide their children to:

- build a larger vocabulary

- compare and contrast qualities among similar items in the same classification

- understand that there is more to know in almost every field of interest

First, identify what it is that you know best. If you begin with your own area of interest and strength, this will be an easier exercise for you. Before you know it, based on your own use of words, your child may be able to identify:

- not just dogs, but golden retrievers, poodles, cocker spaniels, and Jack Russell terriers

- not just flowers, but roses, daffodils, impatiens, irises, and tulips

- not just birds, but egrets, mourning doves, robins, and seagulls

- not just bugs, but spiders, ants, beetles, and millipedes

- not just trees, but eucalyptus, oaks, ash, and pine

- not just breads, but ciabatta, sourdough, pugliese, and baguettes

- not just cars, but Fords, Chevrolets, BMWs, and Volvos

- not just pasta, but macaroni, fusilli, penne, and angel hair

- not just blue, but teal, turquoise, navy, and periwinkle

The important thing to do is capitalize on the fascination with words while your child is young. When children are acquiring vocabulary, they want to learn as many words as possible. In so doing, they engage parents in discussions about the differences and similarities among the different varieties, which calls into play their observational powers.

RETELLING

We develop language by using it. This is especially important for young children who are soaking up new words and phrases every day. One of the techniques used to see how well a child has understood what he has seen, heard, or read is called retelling.

When a child is retelling either a story or a situation, there are many features that we look for. Did he recall the time and place (setting)? Who were the main characters? What did they look like and act like? What was the problem in the story? What were the major events? Were the events told in the proper order? What was the outcome of the story?

As children grow and develop, they increase in sophistication of being able to relay this information.

Retelling can take place in several different formats:

Oral-to-oral

The child has heard a story told to him. He then retells what he has heard. This is one of the first types of retelling used because it does not require the child to be able to read or write.

Oral-to-written

The child hears a story told and then retells it in written form, either with words or in pictures.

Written-to-oral

A child reads a story and then retells it verbally. This is particularly useful when children have been able to master the learning of reading, but writing is still not easy for them.

Written-to-written

By the end of first grade (for many children) and then moving into second grade, children are able to read a story and then write about it.

When they are three to five years old, children are still developing in this area. They may need support from adults in retelling accurately. But as they mature, they should need less and less help in being able to retell events accurately.

FUN WITH STORIES

Try telling a tag team story with your family in the car, around the campfire, at the dining room table, or anywhere else you gather to relax together. One person in the family begins a story with a sentence. Each person takes a turn and adds a sentence when it is her or his turn. It's a fun way to develop listening skills because everyone has to pay attention to each other's story.

FAMILY STORIES

Family stories are an excellent way to pass along the knowledge and values that have made your unique family unit the people they are. Children are enthralled when they hear these tales - especially when they are about their own younger years.

What are the stories that you tell your children? Consider these possibilities:

- The origin of family members' names.
- How your family and/or ancestors came to the United States and then to the area where you are now living.
- How you and other family members overcame adversities and obstacles.
- Your experiences in school and college.
- How you met your spouse or partner, and how the children's grandparents met.
- What life was like when you were a child.
- Your first job.
- What school was like when you were their age.

There are many clear advantages and by-products to conveying these stories to your children:

- It's an excellent way for them to hear oral language. As you tell stories, they learn from your example how a story is put together. This helps them with their expressive language.

- They convey a sense of belonging — to your family, your geographic area, your heritage. This links them, through your family, to others. It engenders a sense of community with those who share a common history.

- They pass on the values that are important to your family. If you want your children to know the value of honesty, trustworthiness, consideration, and perseverance, tell them stories that illustrate these character traits. A parable drawn from real-life experience is a powerful example.

- They place your child in a geographic and historic context. They get the sense of movement from the past to the present by way of hearing about the factors that have brought you and them to the current time.

- They are unique to your family. No television show, movie, or video tells the story of your family. It is something that only you own and share among yourselves.

These stories are an important and integral part of the education that you — and only you — can give your child.

22

FIGURES OF SPEECH

Imagine your child's confusion when she hears about having a chocolate moose for dessert, a gorilla war being fought in another country, somebody being a little pigeon toad, or a person having a frog in her throat. The images don't make sense to young children. How could they be true?

Welcome to the world of figures of speech, idioms, homonyms, and metaphors. They can be especially confusing to young children, who are themselves just coming to grip with the intricacies of the English language.

Language is power. The uninitiated are powerless if they do not understand what they hear. Your child has greater linguistic power if you use figures of speech in your own daily exchanges. The only way to do this is to take the time to sit with and explain what these expressions mean and how they can be confused with other ones. Let's look at an example: the word *reigned* is pronounced exactly like *rained*. Furthermore, your child is more likely to have experienced rain than a monarch's reign. It stands to reason that hearing about a king who reigned for forty years will bring a quizzical look from your young one.

If you yourself are not a native speaker of English, I encourage you to spend some time in this endeavor with your child. It's a fun way for you to learn together about the language.

Children rely on the adults in their lives — mostly parents and teachers — to expose them to vivid and creative language. This is an excellent foothold into linguistic power, and something that parents can help to develop.

PLAYING WITH FIGURES OF SPEECH

There is a delightful series of books that have a marvelous way of illustrating the way children can easily misunderstand figures of speech. *The King Who Rained* (1970) was written and illustrated by Fred Gwynne, whom you may remember from his years as one of *The Munsters* on television. Three other books in the same vein by the same author are *A Chocolate Moose for Dinner* (1976), *A Sixteen Hand Horse* (1980) and *A Little Pigeon Toad* (1988). (All are published by Simon and Shuster.)

MEMORIZING LEADS TO READING AND WRITING

You can have your child's memory for songs and poems reinforce her reading and writing skills. One skill is auditory and the other is visual. They can work together to support each other.

The process from thinking to reading works like this: If you can think it, you can say it. If you can say it, you can write it. If you can write it, you can read it.

Your child, no doubt, knows the words to lots of poems and songs. Ask her to say them to you. If she is in first or second grade, an emergent reader and writer, she may be able to write what she hears.

If she needs help writing, but can say the words to you, write them for her. But only do this after trying to encourage her to sound out the words herself. This is a crucial part of the learning-to-read-and-write process: making the connection between the sound of the letter and the letter itself.

After the words are down on paper, she can "read" them because she can follow along with you as you read them. Help her move her finger from word to word as you read together. In doing this you are re-teaching the flow of reading from left to right.

Having memorized a poem or song means that your child already knows the words. Saying the words while following along with the writing can reinforce the reading process. She observes that each word is distinct and that there are spaces between them.

You can help by going back to the words on the paper and asking such questions as, "What is the first letter of this word? What sound does this letter make?" Guide her through the word letter by letter.

Many times, children memorize the text of beginning and familiar books. This happens in especially fun books that they read with you over and over again. Memorizing lines leads to being able to read the words in isolation.

CHAPTER 2:
READING

When I get a little money I buy books; and if any is left I buy food and clothes.

— Erasmus

HOW DO THEY KNOW WHAT THEY KNOW? BOOKS!

Imagine, if you will, these classroom situations in which individual first-graders had information that none of their peers had:

- I was reading a book to the class. The Eiffel Tower was in one of the illustrations. One of my students knew its name, that it is in Paris, that Paris is in France, and that France is in Europe.

- We read a poem about a chick pecking out of its egg. The poet wonders how it's possible that the chick knows what to do. One of the kids flailed his hand in the air and couldn't wait for me to call on him before he answered, "He probably got it from his mother's DNA."

- When one child asked a question about using wool to make a sweater, one of his classmates gave a detailed description of the process from sheep-shearing to knitting a sweater.

This motivated me to speak to them and their parents to find out how they came by their information. I found out:

- Their homes have lots of books. The parents told me they grew up with lots of books, love books, and they have passed on this love to their children. They teach enjoyment of and respect for books.

- Other reading material at home includes science magazines, newspapers, atlases, and globes.

- They spend a lot of time in the library, reading most of the children's books in their branch.

- They read many books of non-fiction in addition to fiction.

- The parents share their hobbies with their children and discuss the intricacies of these hobbies.

- The children are included in adult conversation about a variety of topics. They do their best to offer answers to all questions that children ask.

The results are a joy to behold. These are children who are self-motivated. They have discovered the rapture that ensues when they are hunting and gathering information. As a teacher, I am all the more excited about teaching them!

BECOMING LIFELONG READERS

Parents are in a powerful position to show their young ones the importance of reading, as well as the value of being lifelong readers.

When we talk about reading, we most commonly think of books. But what about the many other objects around us that require reading? There are menus, newspapers, transit schedules, tax forms, contracts, stock reports, food containers, recipes, graphs, road signs, maps, and instructions for putting things together. Your approach to these, in your child's presence, will be crucial for helping him to see reading as a useful and necessary life skill and tool.

Share this concept with your child: various types of reading work in different ways. For example, when looking up a program in the TV listings, you explain how you have to skim down the left-hand column, passing the hours in chronological order. When looking up a destination on a map, you demonstrate how the alphabetical index works, and then how you match the coordinates given on the map itself to find the destination. When looking at a recipe, you show how there are two parts to it: the list of ingredients and the process you use for putting them together.

Being able to read in these situations will enable you to find the program you want to watch, find the place you want to go, and prepare the food you want to eat. These are valuable motivations for being able to read.

Another important lesson you teach is that you do not have all the answers just because you are an adult. Children think their parents, teachers, and most other adults are omnipotent, that we have it all! We make the rules, not follow them. No wonder that when they play adult roles it includes lots of giving orders to each other!

But it is valuable to get across the idea that adults, just by virtue of being adults, do not have all the answers! We continue to learn, too, as we grow up. And we always will.

LABELING EVERYDAY OBJECTS

Making signs to label common objects around the house is a way to impress upon children that there is a relationship between the words we use to call objects and the letters written on a page.

If you do this, make all lower-case letters, as they are the ones that are most frequently used in writing. Ask you child which items to label. For beginning readers, help sound out words - especially the beginning sounds. The proximity of the word to the object helps with reading and the understanding of the relationship.

The labels can be confined to your child's room or placed around the house, as you wish.

If you like the idea of labeling things so that your child associates the word with the object, but you don't want to do this in your home, consider any one of a number of books that do this same task. Some of them are:

100 First Words to Say with Your Baby, by Edwina Riddell

My First 100 Words in Spanish and English, by Keith Faulkner, illustrated by Paul Johnson.

There are several other *My First 100* and *My First 500 Words* books. Check with your bookstore clerk or librarian for them. The typical format shows scenes such as a kitchen, a living room, a bedroom, a back yard, and a classroom, in which all objects are labeled — some in English and some bilingual books that feature Spanish, French, Russian, Hebrew, and other languages.

CALDECOTT & NEWBERY AWARDS

Perhaps you have seen book covers with insignias that indicate they have won the Caldecott or Newbery Awards. The Caldecott Medal was named for Randolph Caldecott, an English illustrator of children's books. It has been awarded every year since 1938 to the artist of the most distinguished American children's picture book that had been published during the preceding year.

The Newbery Medal was named for John Newbery, an eighteenth century publisher of children's books. It has been awarded annually since 1922 to the author whose books has made the most distinguished contribution to American literature for children.

In looking at these books with your child, it is wise to consider the times during which they were written. Many of us, for example, are familiar with the style of Ezra Jack Keats, whose *The Snowy Day* won the Caldecott Medal in 1963. Keats wrote and illustrated so many books that used his recognizable collage style that from a twenty-first century perspective, we don't necessarily view this as fresh and new. Add to this his African-American character Peter; it was rare to see a children's book featuring a non-caucasian family.

CONCEPTS ABOUT PRINT

There are many things you teach when you read to your child. Teachers call these concepts about print. Among the concepts that you teach are:

- How to handle a book — which side is the front and which is the back.

- How to turn pages.

- The direction in which the print is read.

- The "return sweep," where the eyes go when each line is finished.

- Starting on the left-hand pge and continuing on the right-hand page after the left-hand page is finished.

- Matching words as they are read on the page.

- The meaning that illustrations have, in addition to the words.

READING *TO* YOUR CHILD

The experts agree: reading to your child is the single most important thing you can do to encourage school success. It is also a contributing factor to your child becoming a lifelong learner.

When you introduce reading to your child early on, you are opening new doors to her for the rest of her life. You are introducing her to ways that she can get information, enjoyment, relaxation, adventure, and perspective on the world around her.

There is an additional unseen benefit: it is a loving act of spending time together and giving attention. We've all heard that action speaks louder than words; this is an action that speaks volumes!

READING *WITH* YOUR CHILD

Children love to assert their independence - to show that they can get dressed by themselves, pour their own juice (don't we love that?), and construct their own cities with blocks. If you have started reading to them when they were much younger, before you know it, they will want to read by themselves soon enough. Here are some tips to help make that transition.

- Sit side by side or with your child on your lap. This gives the child the same access to the book that you have as the reader. She sees the same pictures and words that you see.

- Point to words as you read. This is subtle, but it helps you give a lot of important information, such as the direction that you go when you read, the direction the pages are turned, and the punctuation that exists on the page along with the words.

- Use books that your children like and have heard often. Familiarity may be tedious to the adults, but it is wonderful for the children. There is comfort in the predictability of the stories.

- Use books that rhyme, repeat, and have a high degree of correlation between the pictures and the text. This helps children to make a connection between the illustration and the words used to describe it.

- Pause for the children to join in. Once the children are familiar with the story, if you stop and let them chime in, it will help them stay focused and it will keep them thinking. They will also begin to recognize words and phrases - especially the ones that repeat.

- Focus more on fun than on teaching. Your child will be the determiner of how much teaching you will do about words and letters. If he is a reluctant reader, you will probably do less teaching. If he is curious about letters and sounds, you can ask him to point out words and you can explain more to him. Let him take the lead on this.

READ-ALOUD TIPS AND BOOK SELECTION

These are a few ideas that can make this activity enjoyable for adults and children alike:

• Start early. Match the attention span to the length of the book if the child is very young.

• Make it a regular part of your family routine.

• Different levels of books are appropriate for different children. If you have a wide range of ages in the family, it would be best to have separate read-aloud times for individual children or possibly for pairs that are closer in age.

• Books that are written slightly above your child's level are excellent for stretching their intellect and vocabulary.

• For younger children, a high degree of correlation between words and illustration can help them to recognize words as they read.

• Use books that have repeating phrases and sentences. The predictability is comfortable for the emergent reader. It may tend to be boring or monotonous for the adult reader, but you have to realize that the focus of the reading is the child, not you!

• Use funny voices for characters in the stories you read.

• When you find an author that your child likes, get other books by the same author. Read information about the author from the book's cover.

PREDICTABLE BOOKS

If you want your child to join you in reading and to have the sense of accomplishment that she is really learning to read, you can't beat predictable books. These books are so called because there is a pattern that is usually aided by illustrations so that children can tell what is happening. Your librarian can help you to find dozens of these. Some classics are:

Are You My Mother?, by P. D. Eastman

Brown Bear, Brown Bear, What Do You See?, by Bill Martin, Jr.

Have You Seen My Cat?, by Eric Carle

If You Give a Mouse a Cookie, by Laura Numeroff

The Very Hungry Caterpillar, by Eric Carle

Today is Monday, illustrated by Eric Carle

- Special note to dads: since most pre-school and elementary school teachers are women, your reading to your children (and especially to your sons) will heighten the importance of books in their eyes.

- Make sure that your children see you reading on your own, and tell them about the kinds of books and periodicals that you like to read. This is the most visible example to show the importance and value of reading.

- Vary your reading to include non-fiction as well as fiction. This is especially important for boys, as they have a greater interest in non-fiction topics than in fairy tales and other made-up stories.

- Discuss the books after you read them.

- Give your child an opportunity to read to you. Even before the child can read words, the process of telling the story by looking at pictures is great practice for children.

- Reading is a year-round activity - not just during the school week or school year.

- Use books with familiar poems, chants, rhymes, and songs. Once your child has memorized certain selections, use them as a springboard for reading. This is an excellent time to use phonics as a teaching tool. You see the title, "Miss Mary Mack," and you ask your child to show you the words. How do you know that those are the words? There is the "m" sound. You have made an important connection.

- Grab interest. There needs to be some way that the book is interesting to the child: appeals to the sense of fantasy, is funny, teaches about animals that the child likes, has endearing characters, etc. Children need to have a reason to stay with a book and keep coming back to it.

INVALUABLE BOOKS FOR PARENTS

The Read-Aloud Handbook, by Jim Trelease has been updated several times. It contains lots of valuable information for families. In addition to helpful advice about reading aloud, the author chronicles many ways how television adversely affects children's personal growth.

Valerie and Walter's Best Books for Children: A Lively, Opinionated Guide, by Valerie V. Lewis and Walter M. Mayes is filled with books that will keep kids interested in reading.

HELPING EMERGENT READERS

Parents experience a wide range of emotions when they work with their emergent readers. When all is going well, it can be exhilarating. But it doesn't always go well. There is an almost universal standby to which most parents resort when the child is stumped by a word: "Sound it out."

Not all words can be easily sounded out. Here, then, are some strategies that we teachers use:

- Praise for what he did correctly. Notice out loud to your child when he has read words or entire sentences properly. There are times when he will self-correct after making an error; praise him for this, too.

- Check the context for the word. Ask, "Did the word you just read make sense? Does it go with the illustration? Does that word have the letters that go with the word you just said?"

- Give more time. Wait without saying anything while your child sits there and tries to figure it out. The extra moments you give may be just what he needs to figure it out.

- Tell the word and go on. Take the time to go through the letters to explain how this word says what it says. Then move on with the story.

- Reread the sentence, making a substitute sound for the word in question (such as the sound "mmm"). Then go back and see what would make sense in place of that sound.

- Take a look at the word and see if the child can recognize a part of it that appears in other words. For example, if he is stuck on the word *clay,* isolate the *ay,* explaining that it is the same *ay* as in the word *day.* Then rebuild the word with the other letters you have: first the *l* in front of *ay* and then the *c* in front of *lay.*

Most of all, reading together should be a joyous experience. Your child's making too many errors in one sentence is an indication that the book is too difficult. Therefore, make this a book that *you* read to *him*; find another book for *him* to read to *you.*

ELABORATE WHEN READING

One of the strategies that good readers use is elaborating on what they read. Elaboration occurs when readers take newly-gained information and add it to the knowledge base they already have. They sometimes have to take what they have gathered in their reading and use it in another phase of a project that has multiple steps.

Some parents are at a loss as to how they can help their children with assignments that call for this approach. At its core, elaboration involves getting your young reader to talk about the material. It is a way to use social interaction to engage her actively in learning. Here are some specific activities that you can try with your child:

- Take a piece of paper and fold it in half vertically. On the left half of the paper, have her copy word-for-word the passage with which she is working. On the right side, she responds to the passage by asking questions, making personal connections, or interpreting what she has read.

- While reading a work of fiction, the student assumes the role of a character in the story. Stop at the climax so that your child does not know the outcome. Ask your child to take on the mind of the character. Ask him questions to see what he would do next (as that character), thus predicting the outcome of the story.

- While reading a piece of literature, have your child look for words or phrases the author has used that give an indication of what the character is thinking and what her motivations are for her actions. In this way, the young reader becomes a detective and is puzzling together a mystery.

By using these techniques, your child learns to identify the important parts of their texts. The social aspect of the work you do together makes it more meaningful to them.

LOOK-AND-FIND BOOKS

There are many kinds of books that encourage the love of reading, even if children have not yet learned to read independently. The *I Spy* and *Where's Waldo?* books are two of these. Children can look at the pictures for hours at a time.

Where's Waldo books by Martin Handford include *Where's Waldo*, *Where's Waldo Now?*, and *Where's Waldo In Hollywood*.

I Spy books by Jean Marzallo with photos by Walter Wick include *I Spy: A Book of Picture Riddles*, *I Spy School Days*, *I Spy Treasure Hunt*, etc.

Look-Alike books by Joan Steiner use common objects to create familiar scenes and locations. Look for *Look-Alikes* and *Look-Alikes Jr.*

In *Alphabet City* by Stephen T. Johnson, there are photos in which letter shapes are found in common objects in the cityscape. This is a Caldecott Honor Book.

ANTICIPATING MEANING

Children can only make sense of reading when they understand the vocabulary, characters, and situations about which they read.

The main character in *Alexander and the Terrible, Horrible, No Good, Very Bad Day* threatens to move to Australia. This will be meaningless to readers if they do not have some sort of an understanding of what and where Australia is.

A child who has read and understood Cinderella will have a greater appreciation for *Mufaro's Beautiful Daughters*, as the theme is similar, though the setting is Africa.

When you are introducing a new story or non-fiction book to your children, it is wise to anticipate vocabulary or situations that are unfamiliar to them. Handling this before you read to them will heighten the enjoyment of reading together. Introduce these in a discussion before the actual reading, so that the reading of the book can go undisturbed.

It is particularly useful in non-fiction to identify what your child already knows about the topic. This is a good way to prepare for reading. It can also help to determine the level of the book that you are going to choose. If she is interested in spiders, for example, she may already know that they spin webs, have eight legs, and come in several different varieties.

This flip side of the coin gets your child's mind ready to learn. Continuing with the spider example, she may want to find out what they eat, how many eggs they lay, and how long they live. Using this to guide your search for information will aid your choice of reading material.

I usually prefer reading a story straight through the first time I read it to a group of children. There are times, however, when it is hard to resist the temptation to ask, "What do you think will happen next?" or "What *could* happen next?" (It's also a little easier to do this with one child than with a group.)

A child's being able to talk about the possibilities of what will happen in a story indicates his having listened well to what you have read so far. And it is a fine way to take a peek at what is happening in the child's thought process.

FOUR KINDS OF READING

A balanced program in which children learn to read has four different types of reading. More and more classroom teachers recognize the differences among these approaches. I present this to you for two reasons: (1) This can help you to determine if your child's teacher is presenting a balanced program. (2) Parents who reflect this at home can help to give their children the same type of support for reading that they are getting in school.

Reading aloud

The teacher or parent selects a book that is read to the children. The adult does all the reading. Children respond to pictures, meaning, and language in the book. They may join the adult if they know the book well or they may respond to the illustrations, meaning, and language, but they usually do not pay much attention to the print.

Shared reading

In the classroom, the teacher has either a large version of the book (big book) that all the children can see or reads a smaller version of the book while the other children look at their copies. On subsequent readings, as the children get to know the story better, the children usually join in. The adult gives a high level of support. Children can hear each other read and may help each other. If the teacher is reading a big book version of the story, he may use a pointer or ask a child to follow the text with a pointer.

Guided reading

The adult chooses and introduces a new book. She may talk about some of the features (illustrations, concepts the children may not know, situations that will be presented in the book), and does not read the book. A guided reading book will be written at the same level as books the reader has read before. The vocabulary is within reach of the reader. It is up to the child to solve problems of how to read new words. The teacher or parent is there to help, if needed.

Independent reading

Children read individually or with partners. The adult does not have to help in any way. The reader can solve problems throughout the text.

THEY CAN READ WHAT THEY CAN SING

I discovered this when I was a student teacher in 1968, and it still works: kids love to read the words of songs they sing.

By the time a child is five years old, he has memorized the words of many songs. Use that to his advantage by writing down the words and helping him to follow along with them as he sings. Use your finger to point to each word as it is sung.

When I was teaching junior high school English, I had a tough group that usually couldn't wait until the bell rang at the end of the period. But on one particular day, I had typed and copied the words of several Credence Clearwater Revival songs. When the bell rang, the kids were singing and reading; they didn't want to leave until the song was over!

First write the words. This is a springboard for your beginning reader. If you are singing with a CD, use the lyrics sheet that comes with it. Then sing the song together.

Yes, at first your child is singing words that have been memorized. It is true that there may be little or no actual reading. In that respect, it looks like the Whole Language approach to teaching reading.

But you can easily move it to a phonics approach and have your child identify letters that make the sounds he is singing.

Let's say, for example, that you are singing "Mary Had a Little Lamb." Look at the title. Which word is *Mary*? How do you know that? Most children will look at the first letter of the word. It's the only word that starts with *m*. Make the sounds of the other letters in the word. Explain that the *y* frequently makes the *ee* sound at the end of words.

You don't have to go over each word in this way, but you will find that after a while, your child will have shifted from singing words that are memorized to being able to read the words in isolation.

SONGS THAT ARE BOOKS

This is a sampling of songs that have been illustrated as books. My students enjoy looking at these. It is hard to describe the joy that I feel when I observe them, usually in pairs, looking at the book, singing quietly, and following the words with their fingers.

Down by the Bay, by Raffi, illustrated by Nadine Bernard Westcott

Lift Ev'ry Voice and Sing, by James Weldon Johnson, illustrated by Spivey Gilchrist

Love Can Build a Bridge, by Naomi Judd, illustrated by Suzanne Duranceau

Mary Had a Little Lamb, by Sarah Josepha Buell Hale, illustrated by Bruce McMillan

Mary Wore Her Red Dress and Henry Wore His Green Sneakers, by Merle Peek

Miss Mary Mack, adapted by Mary Ann Hoberman, illustrated by Nadine Bernard Westcott

Oh, A-hunting We Will Go, by John Langstaff, illustrated by Nancy W. Parker

Over in the Meadow, illustrated by Ezra Jack Keats

Take Me Out to the Ballgame, by Jack Norworth, illustrated by Alec Gillman

The Star-Spangled Banner, by Francis Scott Key, illustrated by Peter Spier

This Land is Your Land, by Pete Seeger, illustrated by Kathy Jakobson

Today is Monday, illustrated by Eric Carle

LITERARY REFERENCES

What was the most popular phrase of 1999?

I tuned into National Public Radio in December of that year to hear this being discussed. I was particularly curious because I am not very in tune with pop culture and I wondered if I ever would have heard it.

TRY YOUR HAND

Here are ten references and quotations. See if you can pinpoint their origin:

1. I have nothing to offer but blood, toil, tears, and sweat.

2. The land of the rising sun.

3. One if by land, and two if by sea.

4. Et tu, Brute.

5. A journey of a thousand miles begins with a single step.

6. We will bury you.

7. Water, water everywhere, and not a drop to drink.

8. Miles to go before I sleep.

9. I have a dream.

10. My candle burns at both ends.

1. Winston Churchill 2. Japan 3. Henry Wadsworth Longfellow, "Paul Revere's Ride" 4. Shakespeare, Julius Caesar 5. Confucius 6. Nikita Khrushchev 7. Samuel Taylor Coleridge, "The Rime of the Ancient Mariner" 8. Robert Frost 9. Dr. Martin Luther King, Jr. 10. Edna St. Vincent Millay

Finally, there was some agreement: the most popular phrase was, "Is that your final answer?" As I had suspected, I didn't know the point of reference.

It did get me thinking, though. Are parents striking a balance between the culture *du jour* and references from history, geography, and literature that have endured generations? I don't think so. It seems to me that there are many more cultural references to television and movies than to literature.

There are compelling reasons for guiding your child to a higher level of literacy. Chief among them is inspiration. Intelligent people use the language in creative and original ways. Their weaving of words is an excellent example to all who read or listen to them.

Secondly, it is a challenge. Why spend one's life following the easiest course of action?

Thirdly, it is the sign of an educated person — something that sets one apart from the ordinary.

I'm not advocating that children have an education exclusively with references to the classics. We do, after all, live in a vital culture where innovative people are creating in a variety of media. But parents can take care to elevate the level of learning in their families so that television and movies aren't the only cultural reference points for their children.

THE COLLECTOR INSTINCT APPLIES TO BOOKS

What does your child collect? Keychains? Baseball cards? Barbies? Action figures or little stuffed animals?

Use your child's collecting urge to work toward his advantage. When he finds a book he likes, look into other books that the same author has written. Chances are if he liked one, he'll enjoy the author's style in another tome.

One of my favorite authors of books for children is James Marshall. I begin every school year by reading the seven books in the *George and Martha* series, written during the fifteen-year period of 1972-1988. These two lovable hippos exemplify characteristics of a solid friendship: mutual support and appreciation, consideration, occasional scuffles, pranks, and, at the end of the day, always being there for each other. Once my students hear the first one, if I tell them there are more George and Martha books, they want to hear them all.

James Marshall was prolific, and his multiple-books series include Fox, The Stupids, Miss Nelson, and The Cut-Ups. He also re-told several familiar fairy tales in his inimitable style.

In "collecting" and reading the works of authors, help your child look for the elements of style: the same characters appearing throughout, the appearance of the artwork, the themes of the stories told, or the sense of humor of the author.

You get your child to think critically if you ask, "How can you tell that this book was also written by that author?" As your child grows, you are helping her with this skill if you ask such questions as: Why do you think the author wrote this book? How would you have told this story? What changes would you make if you had a chance to write it?

FAVORITE COLLECTIBLE PROLIFIC AUTHORS

Mitsumasa Anno	Steven Kellogg
Frank Asch	Leo Lionni
Marc Brown	Anita Lobel
John Burningham	Arnold Lobel
Eric Carle	David Macauley
Joy Cowley	James Marshall
Donald Crews	Bill Martin, Jr.
Tomi de Paola	Mercer Mayer
Lois Ehlert	Patricia McKissack
Mem Fox	David McPhail
Don Freeman	Robert Munsch
Ruth Heller	Laura Numeroff
Kevin Henkes	Patricia Polacco
Russell Hoban	Allen Say
Tana Hoban	Maurice Sendak
Pat Hutchins	Chris Van Allsburg
Rachel Isadora	Judith Viorst
Ezra Jack Keats	Vera B. Williams

37

FREEDOM OF CHOICE

Freedom of choice: isn't that a fundamental principle of our society? Americans consider this a value of tremendous importance.

Apply this principle to your children's reading material. We are each stimulated by difference sources. Especially at the beginning of the formal school years, there is no telling what will be the key that unlocks reading pleasure for your child.

So many other stimuli have lots of choices: movies, video games, and television are in competition for your child's attention and time. In order for adults to be able to suggest to children that reading is a valid alternative to these other media, they need to have a wide variety of reading materials in their homes and classrooms.

When children are permitted and encouraged to make their own reading choices, they are taking responsibility for their learning process. This is always a positive step. Parents and teachers, therefore, have fewer problems with regard to motivating them to read.

When the occasion comes to give books to children in your extended family, consult your own children for suggestions about their favorites. And don't be shy about asking the recipient about his taste in books. After all, if the toy stores can have registries for toys and games, why not give them a choice in books, too?

Get children into the habit of talking about their choices by promoting a family book talk during dinner on a regular basis. On these occasions, each member of the family talks about a book that she or he has recently read or is currently reading.

During the book discussions, the younger children, while listening to the older ones talk about their book adventures, have goals to which they can aspire as they improve their reading ability. The older children become aware that they are role models for the little ones. And, most important, parents demonstrate their continued interest in using a skill they learned when they were in school.

WORDLESS BOOKS

Many parents are not aware that there are hundreds of storybooks published that have illustrations but no words. Here are six benefits to using wordless books with your children, especially with emergent readers.

- They provide excellent development of oral language. As parent and child look through the book together, they have a conversation about the things they see in the illustrations. Parents help their children to build new vocabulary and strengthen oral language.

- After the story is "read" children can write their own words to go with it. At my school, during a family literacy night, we used 3" x 5" sticky notes for the children and parents to write on. As they finished each sheet, they peeled it off, put it on the page, and continued. Then, when they finished the book, they read together what they had written.

- If you have children of different ages, they can write their own stories at their writing levels, then share the book with the rest of the family.

- They reinforce the important concepts about print, such as how to open a book, how to turn pages, and how the meaning of a book is found in the order of left to right.

- They foster imagination in children. Each child gets to make up his own reasons for the illustrations to be the way they are. There doesn't need to be a "right" or "wrong" version of the story.

- They boost self-confidence in young readers. A child just learning how to read can proudly ask you if you would like to hear him "read" a book. And since he has learned so much that will be valuable in actual reading, this will be very close to being true.

If you are not familiar with this genre, ask your children's librarian for help. Many of them have lists available to give you or can go right to the shelves to pull some for you.

SOME TITLES YOU MAY ENJOY

Anno's Counting Book by Mitsumasa Anno

Anno's Journey by Mitsumasa Anno

Pancakes for Breakfast by Tomie dePaola

Changes, Changes by Pat Hutchins

A Boy, a Dog, a Frog, and a Friend by Mercer Mayer

Peter Spier's Rain by Peter Spier

Deep in the Forest by Brinton Turkle

BOOKS DON'T HAVE TO BE EXPENSIVE

When I talk to groups of parents about the importance of having books in the home, many of them become concerned as they project that this can be a very expensive proposition. It needn't be. Here are some free or inexpensive ways to increase the number of books in your home.

Library

The library is free. Pick one day a week and make it a habit to go to the library every week on that day. Check out the maximum number of books to take home.

Library sales

Many public libraries sell their older books and books that community members donate for that purpose. You can get lots of books for ten cents, twenty-five cents, or a dollar. Check with your library to see how often they do this and when they will do it next.

Garage sales, yard sales, and estate sales

You'll find rock-bottom prices at these events. Stock up!

Hand-me-downs

Ask friends and relatives with children older than yours to pass along the books that their children have finished reading. Then, when your children have finished with them, pass them along in the same spirit.

Used book stores

Head right to the children's section. They will usually have a great selection and reasonable prices.

Thrift shops

Many thrift shops have books in addition to their clothing and household items.

Classroom book clubs

Many teachers subscribe to commercial book clubs that offer very inexpensive books to children. Order forms are distributed by the teacher and the books are mailed directly to the school. In my experience, there are almost always books for less than a dollar.

School fundraising book sales

These are frequently in conjunction with a company that also has book clubs. You will usually find several bargain prices.

Gifts

Are you concerned with the excess of toys that your child has amassed? If so, when a gift-giving occasion is coming up, speak frankly with your relatives or friends who will be purchasing gifts for your child. Request that the gifts be books.

Book exchanges

Round up your kids' friends, invite them all to your home, ask them to bring five books that they don't want any more, and conduct a book exchange among them. Or suggest to the teacher that she do this with the entire class. It's a good way to get new-to-you books flowing through your home.

Book clubs in the mail

Many parenting, women's, and children's magazines advertise clubs in which mailings are sent out monthly. Introductory offers are usually very reasonable — several new books for a dollar.

CHAPTER BOOKS

Many parents understand the joy of reading to their children. The bedtime story is an institution in myriad homes.

There are many reasons to include chapter books in your repertoire when you read to your children.

- This builds listening skills. Since there are usually few pictures, children have to fill in with their own imagination. Television and movies are primarily visual by comparison, so this helps to balance the visual with listening.

- The vocabulary and language are generally very rich. Exposure to new words and ways of putting them together is helpful to young children who are just learning how to read and write.

- It's an activity that families can share and make part of their common experience.

- The best-written stories touch on values many parents will want to reinforce with their children: friendship, courage, adventure, perseverence through adversity, etc.

- It leads to reading as a choice activity for children.

At a presentation I gave to parents, a mom told me that her second grade daughter didn't choose reading as an activity. She wondered if I had an idea to help.

The mom told me that they usually read in bed starting at 8:00 and then turned lights off at 8:30. I suggested that mom choose a chapter book to read to her daughter at bedtime. When 8:30 came, she could offer a choice to the daughter: either turn off the lights and go to sleep or continue reading on her own; if she continued reading, she would be allowed to stay up until 9:00. There aren't many children who can resist the opportunity to delay their bedtime by another half-hour, are there?

The idea worked. Her mom e-mailed me a few weeks later to tell me that her daughter was now hooked on the chapter books. What had begun as a way for the seven-year-old to get away with an extra half hour of being awake transformed into a new way of spending her waking hours during other parts of the day.

POPULAR AUTHORS

Many authors have written excellent chapter books. Some have become so popular that the authors have continued by writing further adventures of their characters, much in the way we read about the Hardy Boys and Nancy Drew when we were younger. Here are some series authors that you may want to look for:

David A. Adler - *Cam Jansen* series

Beverly Cleary - *Henry and Beezus* series; *Ramona* series

Ruth Stiles Gannett - *My Father's Dragon* series

Patricia Reilly Giff - *The Kids of Polk Street School* series

Johanna Hurwitz - *Aldo series; Russell* series

Mary Pope Osbore - *Magic Tree House* series

Peggy Parish - mystery- adventures with Liza, Bill, and Jed

Barbara Park - *Junie B. Jones* series

John Peterson - *The Littles* series

BOOKS ON TAPE

A wonderful way to encourage reading and give beginning readers a boost is to use books on tape. At school, many teachers use these in what we call listening centers. They accommodate several readers at one time. At home, though, you can have either one or several of your children use this technique simultaneously.

Consider these different ways to use books on tape to boost your child's reading:

Many books that are sold these days are also available on audio cassette. As an activity that is purely a listening experience, you could use the cassette so that children can hear the story. You add another learning mode — the visual aspect — when you have the book available as well. That way children can hear the story while they are looking at the book. Many of these cassettes include signals to let young readers know when to turn the page. Audio cassettes are widely available in bookstores, at libraries, and through classroom-based book clubs.

Once your child has experienced a few of these, you may want to branch out a little and be creative with the members of your family. Buying blank tapes gives you the opportunity to make your own stories using the books that you have on hand or borrow from the library. The adults can read the stories, older siblings can read into the microphone, or the newest reader in the family can read. You could even make it a project the entire family can get into, by giving parts to everyone, including the sound effects.

If you have seen Reading Rainbow on television, then you are familiar with the way that stories can come to life on a video cassette. Since many families have camcorders and other means for making home movies, you can also record your family members reading stories this way, either to view at home or to send to grandparents or other family members that will enjoy seeing the kids' reading progress.

BOOK LINKS

The concept of linking kids' interests to books is critical if we are going to see them become lifelong readers and learners. Think about the way that a chain is made. One piece connects to another in a seamless and logical way. Using a similar thought process, we connect one book to another so that the child continues to read more books.

Where does a book link begin? Take your cue from your child's interests and activities. Perhaps a visit to a zoo will spark an interest in one particular animal.

If your child is a sports fan, the beginning of a link can be with a particular player or the sport itself.

A visit to another city, state, or country can be the first of a long link of books about the area.

A book itself can spark your child's interest. We find some way to get that interest and connect it to another book. Was it the author she really enjoyed? The illustrations? The subject matter? Whatever it was, we scour the library for more of the same.

Once you have a subject — spiders, for example — look for other books in which spiders are featured. Non-fiction is an obvious choice, but there are also many story books in which spiders are important characters. *Be Nice to Spiders* and *Charlotte's Web* are two examples. The story of *Anansi the Spider* comes from Africa as a folk legend.

From this point, see if you can continue to link to other books. *Be Nice to Spiders* links the child to reading about bugs, spider webs, and zoos.

Charlotte's Web can lead to farms, pigs, and county fairs.

The Anansi story can lead to life in Africa, other African animals, and other folk tales. Don't be shy about asking your librarian for help in making links among authors' books or to related subjects.

There are many ways to make book links. Among them are:

Author study

If your child likes the works of a particular author, continue to look for other books by the same author.

Single subject links

Your child likes pigs, bears, or dogs. Continue to look for other books in which the main characters are the same. In non-fiction, look for many books about the same subjects: sharks, penguins, South America, etc.

Character links

Your child likes the characters in a particular book: Frog and Toad, Morris and Boris, Arthur, The Cut-Ups, Amelia Bedelia, Arthur, Clifford the Big Red Dog, etc. Look for other books with the same characters.

Topic links

Your child is interested in a particular subject: Africa, for example. The links are almost endless: animals of Africa, people who live there, folk tales and legends, history, current life, etc.

Comparisons of the same story

Some stories are so popular that they have been written by many different authors and in many different cultures. There are many versions of the *Cinderella* story, *The Three Little Pigs*, *Goldilocks and the Three Bears*. Your child can develop higher level thinking skills by reading many variations of the same story and comparing them from one to another.

NATIONAL CHILDREN'S BOOK WEEK IS IN NOVEMBER

"Plant a seed.... Read!"

This was the theme of the 80th annual observance of National Children's Book Week, held from November 15-21, 1999. The purpose of the week is to nurture young people and give them a world view through books.

Children's paths to books are guided by teachers and parents. We teachers are doing what we can to provide opportunities to foster this critical skill. Increased parental involvement on this issue can only benefit children.

Look to your local schools for their effort to elevate the cause of literacy of students in our public schools. Typically, these campaigns hope to increase the level of parent engagement with their children in academic endeavors.

At the elementary school level, effort goes into the building of literacy portfolios for all students. Middle and high school students who are having trouble with their reading can be offered reading intervention classes.

Usually, principals at all school sites are knowledgeable about parent involvement activities. They are the people you may contact to find out what you may do to boost your child's literacy. Look for people who are open to responding to parents' needs, rather than creating a one-size-fits-all approach to boosting literacy and parent involvement.

Here are some suggestions for your next trip to the library or bookstore with your child. Doing these together can serve the dual purpose of expanding her or his literacy as well as establishing your interest in reading. See if you can find:

- a new book by an author you already know

- a book by a new-to-you author

- a new book on a subject you enjoy

- a new version of a fairy tail or legend that you enjoy

- a book about another culture

- a book in a genre you haven't read yet: mystery, adventure, biography, biology, geography, sports

For a wealth of online information, see the Children's Book Council website at www.cbcbooks.org

READING THE NEWSPAPER

Many households have on hand a tool that can be an enjoyable resource for your child: the newspaper.

The newspaper is a fine example of teaching children to read for a purpose. Once children understand what can be found inside it, they can look through it to find information that is useful to them.

Make a treasure hunt out of it. See if your child can find various items that are common to the newspaper. First of all there is always a variety of news stories. See if you can find:

- a story about a person who helped somebody else

- a story about your own city

- a story about an animal

- a cartoon or comic strip

- a letter to the editor

- a photo with lots of action

- a photo with athletes

- a headline that makes the story sound interesting

- stories from other parts of the country or from other countries

If the information you find in a newspaper piques your child's interest in some way, use this as a jumping-off point for a trip to the library or a supervised search on the Internet, where there will be ways to find out more information on the same subject.

Names of other countries or cities that show up in the newspaper can lead to getting out a map and showing your child where these places are.

There is frequently news that is controversial in some way. This can be an opportunity to explain your values and perspective to your child. Children need to know where their families stand on such issues. It is a way that they begin to form opinions of their own. By all means, use the conversation to have them explain their opinion to you. Being able to express themselves is a fine way to clarify their feelings for themselves.

If your child feels strongly enough about an issue, it would be a great opportunity to express himself by writing a letter to the editor.

READING DURING THE SUMMER

No more pencils, no more books, no more teachers' dirty looks!

We sang that on the last day of school about a hundred years ago. I hope that parents won't let kids take the "no more books" seriously.

Summer is a great time to keep up reading skills and make sure that the kids don't lose any of the hard-earned progress gained during the school year.

Check to see if your local library has an enriching summer reading program. Be careful, though, in your use of summer reading lists that some school districts disseminate. These can create hardships for libraries.

The greatest problem is that parents flock to the library for listed books, which are usually in limited supply. They check them out, keep them for as many as four weeks, and make it difficult for others to get them. In the process, they ignore many of the other fine books that the libraries have on hand.

Librarians suggest that you look for the shelf of new books. Since most libraries have limited funds for purchasing books, they do so based on careful considerations from many sources. The shelf of recently acquired books is, in and of itself, a suggested reading list.

It is always best to have kids choose reading on the basis of its being a good use of time. This is intrinsic motivation. But not all kids work that way; some of them need a little nudge to get them to read. Just in case your child needs some extrinsic motivation, see if the successful completion of your library's summer reading program will net each child any of the prizes that are sometimes available, such as free ice cream, pizza, tickets to a baseball game, and perhaps books. Stop by your branch library to sign up.

Kids who read during the summer maintain their reading skills when the new school year begins. Secondly, when children are empowered to set their own goals, there is a greater chance that they will attain them.

Katy Obringer, Supervisor of Children's Library in Palo Alto, has forwarded me the findings of a study by Barbara Heyns, who wrote *Summer Reading and the Effects of Schooling* (published in 1978, now out of print).

Working with 1,493 sixth-graders, Heyns determined that:

- the number of books read over the summer was a significant predictor of gains in reading over the summer.

- those who read more than six books over the summer gained more than those who read fewer than six books.

- children who used the library read more than those who did not.

- those who lived closer to the library read more.

CHAPTER 3:
WRITING

If you wish to be a

writer, write.

— Epictetus

GETTING READY TO WRITE

The muscles in little fingers need lots of preparation if the child to whom they are attached is going to be comfortable writing.

Several activities that are not even related to writing can be helpful in getting small hands ready for the task. Manipulation of clay, playdough, and polymer clay is a strengthening exercise for the fine muscles.

Building with blocks can also be a significant boost to this skill. As soon as the danger in swallowing small pieces is gone (usually by the age of four, but this may vary with the child) interlocking pieces such as Legos and LinkerCubes are a fine next step. They demand a greater degree of control and manual dexterity that helps to strengthen finger muscles.

Stringing beads, tying shoelaces, and manipulating buttons, zippers, and snaps on clothing are other activities that help to work these muscles.

A variety of crayons, markers, and pencils can provide your budding writer with a non-threatening experience. Provide ample time to practice drawing.

After drawing objects, and when children are aware that letters and words have meaning, they will naturally want to label what they have drawn.

For the reluctant writer, parents can help make the bridge to writing by taking the child's dictation. Children who tell a story and then watch as an adult writes the words are learning that their words are given special meaning when they are written. This can be an incentive for most children, who want to be like the adults and older siblings who model this task.

One of the pitfalls of this activity is approached when we are dealing with a child who is a perfectionist. This child doesn't want to do something unless it is right; he is afraid of making mistakes. This is the point at which the caring adult can explain that this is a process that takes years to perfect. Explain, in a very matter-of-fact way, that making mistakes in writing is not a problem — that everyone makes them. And, above all, that mistakes are a tremendous opportunity for learning.

SPELLING

The approach to teaching spelling has changed since today's parents were learning to write. One of the most significant differences is the acceptance of what teachers call "invented" or "temporary" spelling. Acceptance of this approach to spelling has been increasing during recent years.

There are several advantages to having children use invented spelling:

- They write more freely and creatively. With less emphasis on spelling during the first draft, they can get their creative ideas onto the paper.

- They are not limited to using only the words they know how to spell. A first-grader, for example, certainly knows what a vacation is. But she probably doesn't know how to spell the word. This way, she can write about it and, during the revision process, after her thoughts are down on paper, learn how to spell the word properly.

- We recognize the simple fact that children's knowledge of oral language is significantly greater than their knowledge of written language. This gives them an opportunity to make the transition from oral to written language. Just as we know that they do not pronounce new words correctly the first time(s) they say them, we also understand and accept that they do not spell every word correctly at first, and we do not assign a penalty to this.

- If we were to expect that children would write only words that they know how to spell, therefore writing without any errors, they would have to use a much more limited number of words. They, therefore, would not be able to express their complex ideas using a limited writing vocabulary.

The teacher looks beyond spelling mistakes in favor of understanding the message the young writer is trying to get across. Overly focusing on how to spell words during the early writing stage may derail the child's creativity.

This is a natural progression in writing. Editors work with writers at the end of the writing process, rather than at the beginning. First the writer has to have something to say.

This response mirrors the one that parents make when a baby is learning to speak. When a toddler picks up an empty cup and says, "oos," a parent doesn't say, "Now wait a minute. If you want juice, you are going to have to practice making that "j" sound."

Rather, the parent accepts the approximation, understanding that learning to speak takes several years. During that time, the child will have many opportunities to hear people say *juice* correctly and that she will learn how to say it as they do. In the meantime, the parent is proud that the child has communicated what she wanted.

50

Similarly, a child writing a story may not know how to spell *friend*. Many teachers will encourage beginning writers to say the word slowly and write down the sounds that they hear. If the child does this, she will likely write "frnd" on his paper.

The teacher wants to strengthen a crucial concept to the emergent writer: the relationship between the written symbol on the page (the letter) and the sound that it makes.

Later, while editing, the teacher points out missing or incorrect letters. It's also a good time to teach about spelling conventions.

In addition, the teacher has the same confidence about the child's learning to spell that the parent had about her learning to speak: that she will be exposed to the word *friend* many times in future reading, and will come to incorporate its proper spelling in her own writing.

There are several ways that parents can help with spelling among their new writers. First and foremost, parents approach this in a supportive way so that children are willing to take risks without being overly concerned about perfection or failure. In order to do this, parents should:

- provide an encouraging environment with a variety of writing tools, paper, letters, alphabet and picture books.

- read often to their children. Good literature is the best model for children when they take up the pen(cil) themselves.

- answer questions about writing. Instead of giving the spelling for specific words, help children sound them out. When learning to write, children need a stronger sense of the relationship between what they hear and the way the letters look. Teachers call this the sound-symbol relationship.

- emphasize meaning over correct spelling. This means that there will be more concern about what the writer means than about how words are spelled. Too much emphasis on correct spelling reverses this.

- accentuate the positive. Notice to your child what she is doing correctly, instead of what is being done incorrectly. With this approach, children will learn that they will improve with practice.

- provide opportunities for authentic writing. If writing is going to be seen as having a purpose, there must be reasons to write. Have your budding writer write the shopping list, signs for things around the house, letters or e-mails to family members, and original stories, plays, songs, or poems.

- help children to become aware of proper spelling. Word games are excellent at this. Point out patterns in words (see the list of rimes on page 53). Play Scrabble or other words games. The knowledge that older siblings have will frequently encourage younger ones with an attitude to succeed.

KINDERGARTEN AND FIRST GRADE SPELLING LISTS

Here are some words that the typical kindergartner and first-grader should be able to spell by her/himself by the end of those school years:

KINDERGARTEN

a	am	and	at	cat
dog	go	I	in	is
it	like	my	no	see
the	to	up	we	zoo

FIRST GRADE

after	all	are	as	ask
ball	be	big	both	boy
but	by	call	came	can
car	come	dad	day	did
do	eat	fall	far	find
for	get	going	got	had
has	have	he	help	her
him	his	hold	if	into
jump	just	kind	last	let
look	lot	love	man	maybe
me	men	mom	morning	much
must	next	not	old	on
or	out	over	play	put
ran	red	run	said	same
say	she	short	shout	small
so	some	stop	sun	swim
tall	tell	that	them	then
they	thing	this	today	told
too	took	toy	under	upon
us	was	went	will	with
yes	yet	you		

RIMES

English is not known for its regularity. Therefore, when teachers find something that can be made regular, we latch onto it as a teaching tool.

One of these tools is a list of rimes, referred to as *chunks* by some teachers and also called *phonograms*, a vowel sound plus a consonant sound which needs an initial consonant or blend to make it a word.

When children understand that these groups have the same sound wherever they read them and the same spelling whenever they write them, they can learn many words with very little additional effort.

Working together with these rimes can lead not only to increased reading, spelling and writing independence, but to an enhanced vocabulary for children. You can turn it into a game for learning new words.

When working with small groups of students, I give clues about the word so that children can guess what it is. They also try to lead each other and me to guess their words that include the rime.

I was recently working with a small group, using the chunk *ank*. Some of the clues I gave were: It's a place where people go to get money. It's what a boat did when it went underwater. It's what you do when you pull something away from somebody quickly.

This process can shed a light on the way children hear. One of them gave as his clue, also for the rime *ank*, "It's something that you can eat." Nobody was able to guess what it was, so we asked him to tell us. His word was *cake*. I had to explain that *cake* did not rhyme with *bank*, *sank*, and *yank*.

Note that the rime can appear anywhere in the word. Thus *Frankenstein*, and *cranky* are also acceptable answers for words that have *ank* in them.

You may find that working with magnetic letters on a cookie sheet or the refrigerator door is a fun way to work with these. That way, the rime can stay in place and other letters around it can be moved around easily.

This list of 37 rimes can yield nearly five hundred words that can be read by children in primary grades:

ack	ick
all	ide
ain	ight
ake	ill
ale	in
ame	ine
an	ing
ank	ink
ap	ip
ash	ir
at	ock
ate	oke
aw	op or
ay	ore
eat	uck
ell	ug
est	ump
ice	unk

Beginning to Read: Thinking and Learning About Print, by Marilyn J. Adams, Cambridge: MIT Press, 1990.

TYPES OF WRITING

In the primary classroom, most teachers typically provide four different types of writing experiences for their students. I think that it is important for parents to know what is happening at school, so that they can give similar support at home for writing. We can expect more progress and success when we are all working together toward a common goal.

These different types of writing differ in their use and in the amount of support that is given by the adult to the child.

Shared writing

The teacher does the writing in a group setting, which is usually the entire class, but may be a smaller group. The teacher helps the children to put the words together in a meaningful way. Usually phrases and sentences are reread many times during this process, so that the lesson also becomes a reading lesson. The most important aspect of this process is that the teacher is showing the children how their ideas can be written down on paper.

Interactive writing

The teacher is very active and supportive, doing most of the writing, but does call up children to share the pen or marker, usually for the most phonetic words that children will be able to sound out easily. All children are involved in providing words, thoughts, and sentences. It is a shared piece that belongs to everyone.

Guided writing

The students select their own topics and the teacher is available for guidance and response during the writing. There can be individual or group conferences, during which the teacher may call together a group of children that may be having similar problems with their writing, such as the use of capital letters, the possessive, or punctuation.

Independent writing

Children are on their own or working together, without support from an adult. Children put together their own sentences and spelling. If they need a word, they know where to look - word wall, picture book, dictionary, calendar - so that they can get their needed words without adult help.

THE WRITING PROCESS

Many teachers use a multi-step process to help children learn the fine art of writing. It's not every written piece that goes through this, but it is a good idea for children to learn that attention needs to be paid to process, and not just to the end product.

Keep in mind as you read the following that not every piece of writing will go through every one of these stages. This is primarily a method for helping new writers to be patient with both writing and themselves so that, as they develop in this area, they can take pride in their work.

Pre-write

This is the time when the writer gathers ideas about the writing to be done. It may begin with drawing a picture or chart, listing the sequences of the story, making notes, jotting down plans, or doing some other sort of diagram. This can be done by the writer himself or in discussion with others.

Draft

The emphasis in this stage is to get ideas down on paper. To keep ideas and creativity flowing, there is not a lot of attention being paid to spelling, grammar, and punctuation during this phase of the process.

Share

After the first draft, the writer gets together with somebody else who can hear what has been written. At school, it is a classmate; at home it can be a sibling or parent. During this process, the person who hears the story for the first time may have something important to tell the writer: perhaps words have been left out or there is something that does not make sense. This is a good time to clear up misunderstandings.

Revise

Having heard the response from others, the writer can now make revisions so that words are better chosen and it flows better.

Edit

Now is the time to spell words correctly and make sure that the writer is using proper punctuation and grammar. The sequence of events in the story is made more clear.

Publish

The world is ready to see what the writer has written. The format can vary. It could be the final form of a card, letter, or creative story. In school, it may go into the classroom library or school library. At home, it may be available for other family members to read. It could also be sent to a loved one out of town.

Confer

Talk with the author about his work. This is a good time for encouragement!

MAKING & WRITING YOUR OWN BOOKS

A Book of One's Own: Developing Literacy Through Making Books, by Paul Johnson, illustrated by Jayne Restall, is a guide to making books and how they foster your child's literacy skills.

Bookworks: Making Books by Hand, by Gwenyth Swain, is a treasure trove of information about making books, including the history of books, making paper, binding, and several different formats of books.

If you don't want to go through the process of folding the paper and making the book, contact Treetop Publishing, makers of Bare Books, which are bound and assembled with durable high-quality blank paper between hard covers. There are several sizes available, as well as covers that are blank and illustrated. For their catalog, call 800-255-9228 or visit them at their website, www.barebooks.com.

PROOFREADING CHECKLIST

Following is a list that you can use at home to have your child go over her writing after it has been written.

1. I started each sentence with a capital letter.
2. I put a space between the words.
3. I started new paragraphs where appropriate.
4. I indented for new paragraphs.
5. I used correct punctuation.
6. I used complete sentences.
7. I used my best spelling.
8. I used descriptive and interesting words (details).
9. I capitalized the important words.
10. In the case that I have written a story:
    a. There is a beginning, a middle, and an end.
    b. I told the story in a logical order.
    c. If there is a problem in the story, I explained it in a way that the problem was solved.

FAMILY PEN PALS

Remember the thrill of receiving mail when you were a kid? I do!

Keep your family connections going, wherever the kids' grandparents, cousins, aunts and uncles live by providing opportunities for your children to write to their far-off relatives and friends.

With the e-mail connections that many of us have, it is easy keep in touch over the miles. Your children are budding writers, too, so include them in the process. But e-mail doesn't offer the same variety afforded by traditional mail.

"I'm sending your school photo to Aunt Zelda and Uncle Roscoe in Oshkosh," you tell your little ones. "Let's put in letters and drawings to cousins Ike and Mamie, too." The family sits down to communicate with their cousins.

Perhaps a relative with time on her hands can write regularly to your kids. The children learn that writing has a purpose, and can send a story or picture to them to keep up the relationship.

In addition to the short note that is going out now, maybe you can include a photocopy of the latest book report, science fair project, or original story written at school. Once the ball gets rolling, you will find lots of things to send along.

If a constant correspondence between two households is not what you care to do, set up a circular route through which material is mailed. You mail to the cousins in Buffalo, they add to it and send it off to Bradenton, then it goes on to Phoenix and Monterey before it comes back to you. Each time you get it, you take out your oldest piece(s) and send along something new. Promise each other that you will put something in the mail within a week after you receive your envelope.

No matter how much is able to be sent from one household to another by e-mail, the kids will appreciate it much more when you announce, "You've got mail," than when the mechanical voice on the computer does it.

Consider the following points if you would like to have your children contribute to family correspondence:

- Preschoolers and kindergartners may not have a handle on letter formation; nor will some of them be able to write their names. We encourage their scribbles, call it "writing," and praise their inclusion in the process. This sets the tone for future positive attitudes about writing.

- By the middle of the year, most first-graders can write several coherent sentences.

- Second- through fifth-graders can write a paragraph to update correspondents about their lives. Their nascent art skills give any note a touch of personality.

57

- If you have a computer, that may make the job easier. If notes are mass-produced, be sure to add some artistic touch to personalize it for each recipient.

By including your children in the process of writing to others, you have several equally important concepts to put into motion: you are valuing your child's contribution to your activities, spending enjoyable family time together, and placing a value on the importance of writing.

KEEPING IN TOUCH

A guide to help children with popular words and phrases for writing cards and letters to family and friends.

DEAR...

aunt	little
auntie	uncle
big	ma
brother	mama
cousin	mom
dad	mommy
daddy	mother
father	pa
friend	papa
grandfather	pops
grandma	principal
grandmother	secretary
grandpa	sister
granny	step-father
	step-mother
	teacher

WISHING YOU...

Congratulations
Get well soon.
Happy birthday to you.
Happy Chanukah
Happy Father's Day
Happy Halloween
Happy holiday
Happy Kwanzaa
Happy Mother's Day
Happy New Year
Happy Thanksgiving
Happy Valentine's Day
How are you?
I like you.
I love you.
I miss you.
Merry Christmas
Please come to my party.

YOU ARE...

amazing
awesome
best
cool
dynamite
excellent
extraordinary
fabulous
far out
first rate
good
great
great example
greatest
impressive
incredible
joy
marvelous
most beautiful
nice
outstanding
phenomenal
pretty
sensational
shining
star
special
spectacular
superb
terrific
thoughtful
tremendous
unbelievable
unique
winner
wonderful

59

VALENTINES: AN EXAMPLE OF AUTHENTIC WRITING

With most teachers allowing classroom time for the exchange of valentines, this is a project that helps children to see that writing has a purpose.

If you have either a computer or easy access to a copy machine, encourage your child to design and copy her own cards. With a message created one time, all that is left to be added are the greeting and signature.

Alternatively, and especially for children in the intermediate grades (3-5) put out a variety of paper, markers, and glue or glue stick and let their imagination take over. If your primary (K-2) student is motivated and able to do this, that would be great, but it may be a mistake to expect that she can do this by herself.

Resist your temptation to address or write the cards yourself. This is a process that most children can do by themselves. And if the task is too daunting to be done in one sitting, you can approach it by breaking it up into several days. A few cards done each day may be a better approach for your child.

The important social lesson to teach at this time is that everyone in the class receives one of your child's cards. I always tell parents of my students to take the all-or-nothing approach: either everyone gets a card or nobody does. In elementary school, this is an expression of friendship, not passion.

If you decide to go the buy-it-by-the-box route with the theme collection that includes one for the teacher (don't forget the teacher!), you can still have your child create cards for out-of-town relatives. They would appreciate your child's thoughts and originality.

SUMMER SCRAPBOOK

Here's a project that develops literacy skills along with artistic flair: a scrapbook to chronicle your child's summer adventures.

Wherever she spends the summer and whatever she does, there's almost no end to the amount of mementos that can be combined with photos and diary-style writing to produce a volume that will be treasured for years to come.

The first thing that comes to mind for most of us when we think of scrapbooks is photographs. You'll probably be taking lots of them this summer anyway, as activities head out-of-doors for swimming, hiking, picnicking, and other events. You're in luck. Many film processors these days include a second set of prints at no extra charge. Keep one for the family album (or, if you're as chronically behind as most people, that overstuffed shoebox in your closet or drawer), and give the other set to your child for her scrapbook.

Once you get into the habit of thinking about the scrapbook, it will be easy to remember to save other odds and ends for inclusion: ticket stubs, flyers, post cards, you-name-it.

The amount of writing done by your child will depend on her age and writing skill. The very youngest of kids can dictate their stories. Older kids can and should write more on their own to keep this skill fresh. If you want to replicate the school approach to writing, help your child to understand the process of first writing a rough draft, then editing and rewriting her words for the final product.

The artistic side comes into play when all the components are laid out on the pages. Kids can also add their own drawings, either mounted or written directly on the pages.

I end with a note about preserving this work. Just as you would do for your other photo albums, make sure that you use only acid-free and lignin-free paper for this album. Avoid the "magnetic" peel-off plastic sheets that destroy photos over time. I use and recommend the line of Creative Memories products that have been designed with creativity and longevity in mind.

a	like	day	friends
the	then	out	too
and	were	him	other
I	all	will	after
to	go	not	don't
was	get	people	our
my	there	make	no
of	with	could	just
we	had	or	has
he	are	can	lot
it	so	very	fun
they	went	play	things
would	up	some	by
is	at	what	little
in	said	this	know
have	them	time	want
that	if	home	saw
for	her	good	did
you	one	as	more
she	because	down	see
be	do	their	big
on	school	house	us
but	got	back	your
when	his	came	every
me	about	from	didn't

CHAPTER 4:
MATH

$+^5 \frac{=}{7} \frac{7}{\div} \times_3$

You are a

mathematical genius

in disguise.

— Marilyn Burns

PATTERNS

Patterns are all around us. Bricks in a walk, stripes or plaid in clothing, and trees planted in orchards are examples of the way people have placed patterns into their environments.

Patterns are the basis of mathematics. Children's ability to identify, duplicate and create patterns outside of math underlies the comprehension of numeric patterns. These activities lead to greater comfort with and understanding of math.

The approach to teaching math has changed significantly in the last ten years. First-graders used to have early exposure to the math problems that their parents recognized: pages of exercises with kids adding 2 + 4 and the like. Unfortunately — and I remember this well — the kids didn't understand what they were doing. How could they be expected to add 7 and 5 if they couldn't grasp what these numbers meant?

In today's kindergarten and first grade classrooms, teachers spend a significant amount of time working with children to recognize and create patterns. With this as a foundation, by the time they get to the traditional addition and subtraction problems, the kids know what they are doing!

When your child counts to 100, help her to recognize the patterns: how the sequence of 1, 2, 3, 4, 5, 6, 7, 8, 9, and 0 repeats itself in the ones place as well as in the tens place. Also notice the different sequences that show up when counting by 2, 5, 10, 25, and 50.

For most children, this is an auditory process. A chart of the numbers from 1 to 100 is a good tool for children who are visual learners. For kids learning multiplication, an old-fashioned chart, with the multipliers across the top and down one side and the products in the middle gives a depiction of patterns.

Asking your child to explain what she sees is a good way to help with the understanding of the patterns. As with so many aspects of learning, if we can express our understanding to another person, it helps us to understand it ourselves.

NOTICING NUMBERS

How many times have you caught yourself saying, "I was never any good in math"? Don't pass on this negative attitude to your children!

Comfort with numbers at an early age can help to build confidence in math and lead to an enthusiasm that will stay with children throughout their lives. It is also a precursor to a successful job!

Start with very young children by noticing numbers wherever you go together. Look at all the vehicles on the road for license plates and telephone numbers. Billboards, buses, street signs, and houses also have numbers.

In the grocery store, take the focus off of the items that your children want to buy (all that stuff you don't want!) and put them on a treasure hunt. One trip can fulfill needs of different ages of children in the same family:

For the youngest, who are becoming aware of numbers, show what a particular number looks like and have her find it on the prices on the shelves. A first-grader who has a better grasp of what numbers mean will be able to compare numbers and answer, "Which one costs more?" when shown two items with different prices.

For the child in the intermediate (third-fifth) grades, give a greater challenge such as asking, "If this costs 79 cents, how many of them would I be able to buy with two dollars? Three dollars? Four dollars? Children of this age can learn to estimate, calculate without pencil and paper, and do math problems like this with the use of a calculator. With your encouragement, they now have countless possibilities of things to do in the grocery store. Older children can help the younger ones on their treasure hunts, thereby reinforcing their own knowledge of numbers and what they represent.

In spending time with your children this way, you are showing them that there are learning opportunities wherever you go, that you are interested in their learning, that math can be fun, and that they can work together to find solutions to real-life math problems.

MATH VOCABULARY

Parents who use math vocabulary when speaking with their children help them to have a better basis for understanding math concepts. If you know the meaning of these terms, use and explain them when you use them. If there are some that you don't know, find out what they mean and make an effort to incorporate them into your speech and activity.

Helping a child to feel secure in math is easier done when he is younger.

shapes: circle, triangle, rectangle, square, rhombus, parallelogram, hexagon, octagon, pentagon, sides, line, point, round

three-dimensional shapes: sphere, cube, pyramid, polyhedron, dome, ball, obelisk, geometry

fractions: half, third, quarter, fifth, sixth, seventh, eighth, ninth, tenth, etc.

decimals: percent, decimal point

cardinal numbers: one, two, three, etc.

ordinal numbers: first, second, third, etc.

number sense: numeral, digit, integer, pattern, next, figure, number sequence, counting, even, odd, every other, infinite, infinity, calculate

measuring, imperial system: inch, foot, yard, square foot, cubic foot, mile, square miles, acre, bushel, peck,

measuring, metric: centimeter, millimeter, meter, kilometer, hectare

measuring liquids, imperial: cup, ounce, pound, half-pint, pint, quart, gallon, barrel

measuring liquids, metric: liter

time: second, minute, hour, day, week, month, year, decade, century, millennium, annual, anniversary, biannual, centennial, sesquicentennial, bicentennial, calendar

math functions: add, plus, subtract, minus, multiply, times, divide, number sentence, equation, answer, sum, difference, product, result, least to greatest, greatest to least, missing, most like, the most, the least, square root, pi

money: cent, dollar, penny, nickel, dime, quarter, half-dollar, dollar

comparisons: the same as, less than, fewer than, more than, equal to, as many as

recording: graph, axis, point, chart

geometry: point, line, angle, obtuse, right angle,45°, 90° 180°, 360°

MONEY JAR

In my classroom, we have a little jar into which I put a penny for each day of school. When we have ten pennies, we trade them for a dime. In this way, I am, among other things, introducing the concept of place value — tens and ones, with the dimes representing the tens and the pennies as the ones.

It was through this process that I realized many of my first-graders do not know one coin from another. There are many activities that families can do with just a handful of coins.

A good beginning activity for the youngest children is to have them sort coins, putting together the ones that are the same. In this type of exercise, the vocabulary will be centered around the size and colors of the coins, as well as the names that we use to refer to each one: penny, nickel, dime, quarter, half-dollar, and dollar.

Next, children can begin to understand the value of each coin. Once this is firm in your child's mind, you can introduce a new type of counting. This is the time for children to understand that you can count how many *dimes* you have when you count by 1: 1, 2, 3, 4, 5 dimes. But when you count how much *money* you have, you count by 10: 10, 20, 30, 40, 50 cents.

Counting by 5, 10, 25, and 50 may be a challenge at first, but it is a skill that helps children to understand the underlying principle that mathematics is based on patterns. When children begin to understand these patterns, they have a better grasp on math.

Through the coins, parents can teach children about the people who are depicted on them: Presidents Lincoln, Jefferson, Washington, Roosevelt, and Kennedy, as well as Susan B. Anthony and Sacajawea.

In 1999, the United States Mint began introducing new quarters every ten weeks. There will eventually be a design on the reverse to honor each state. This is a fine way to talk about the states and introduce them to children.

By keeping a bunch of coins handy you can teach lessons from basic math to geography.

NUMBER PAIRS AND TRIADS

The idea of number pairs and triads in math helps kids to make sense of the work they are doing.

The youngest of children understand that $5 + 5 = 10$. This is a good place for you to start because it is easy to see and, therefore, concrete: five fingers on one hand plus five fingers on the other hand equals ten fingers altogether.

A next big step comes with the understanding that numbers can be paired differently to make ten. Thus, children learn the various pairs $(1 + 9, 2 + 8, 3 + 7,$ etc.). Ten, the third number that makes these triads, is a building block of math in many cultures, so it is a good piece of information to understand.

A solid understanding of addition generally precedes that of subtraction. Help your child to see that the same pairs in an equation such as $7 + 3 = 10$ can be manipulated to make two subtraction equations: start with 10, subtract one of those numbers (3) and the answer is the other number (7).

Once your child begins working with multiplication, the same principle is true when you compare multiplication and division equations. Take the three numbers, manipulate them, and you can turn multiplication triads into division triads: $9 \times 7 = 63$ becomes $63 \div 7 = 9$.

In working with your youngsters this way, they must thoroughly understand concrete examples before they move on to abstract ideas with numbers. In recognizing this, you help to ensure that they are not just parroting answers to you; there is true understanding behind what they are saying.

Above all, try to find ways for math games to be an enjoyable activity with your children. For example, a first grade teacher colleague tells me that she used to play a game called Contact with her grandmother. In that game, the challenge was always to come up with combinations of numbers that added up to 15. As a result, she had an enjoyable time playing with her grandmother and she has always maintained that solid understanding of these combinations.

USING A CALCULATOR

Kids love playing with gadgets. If you use a calculator to help balance your checkbook or any one of a number of other activities, explain to your child what you are doing. Hand over the calculator for a while and have him push the buttons. Even when children are saying nonsense numbers like "sixty-five hundred billion trillion," they are showing an interest in math. Use that interest to teach.

CALENDARS

Any time is a good time to get your child his own calendar — especially if you are looking for one after the beginning of the calendar year when stores are selling them at 50% off the original price.

Spend some time going through the calendar with your child. Depending on his knowledge of what's in the calendar, this is a good time to go over calendar terms such as the names of the days of the week, the months of the year, the seasons, and such concepts as yesterday, today, tomorrow, next week, next month, etc.

If you have a centralized place where you keep such information as the birthdays of people in your family, anniversaries, school vacations, family trips, and other events, help your child get these dates noted on his own calendar. Children often have invitations to lots of their friends' and classmates' parties. These go on their calendar, too.

Your writing will be neater and more presentable, but your child will have a greater ownership of the calendar as his tool if the writing on it is his. And if there are days that he deems as important, let him be the judge of those. After all, it's his calendar.

Lead your child to ability in using his calendar by guiding him through using it, instead of giving the answers outright. If he wants to know how much more time it will be until a certain event, use what I call sharing your thinking out loud. For example, if he asks how long it is until Halloween, you would go through the calendar with him and your comments may be something like this: "It's now the middle of January, so until the end of the month is half a month. Then there's February, so that's one and a half; then March, so that's two and a half," etc. You continue until you show that Halloween is nine and a half months away.

In so doing, your child gets counting skills, calendar awareness, and gets a handle on the passage of time.

TELLING TIME

How long will it take to get there? How long until 2:00? How much time does it take to make the bed?

Kids have fuzzy concepts about time. These concepts will stay that way until we do something to clear them up.

How many times have you reminded your child to make his bed, pick his clothes up off the floor, or brush his teeth, just to notice that he still hasn't begun to do the required task? I've noticed that, for some reason, both at home and at school, kids get movin' when I start counting or timing them. I don't know why it works, but it usually does.

Instead of nagging about doing the task you are talking about, try saying, "Okay, let's see how long it takes you to make that bed. Ready, set, go!" And then watch the second hand keep track of the time for you.

Interpreting the results can be helpful. This is how you find out that it takes only one and a half minutes to make the bed, five minutes to take out the garbage, or two minutes to straighten up the bathroom after the bath.

Children start to understand how long a minute is because their activities are measured by using this unit.

I also like this method because we adults can use it we can help children understand that their time is a contribution that needs to be made to help family life flow smoothly. They are the beneficiaries of the hours that we spend cooking, cleaning, shopping, and maintaining things around the house. It is, therefore, reasonable that we expect them to spend their five minutes here and ten minutes there as a contribution meant to help the family.

As with so many things, a lesson begun with teaching time and its meaning becomes a lesson about the understanding of what it takes to keep things running smoothly when all members of the family pitch in and contribute their share.

MEASURING

Whether you use metric or imperial measurements, familiarizing your child with measuring tools and the process can give her a boost in understanding the meaning of numbers.

You probably have extra sets of measuring cups, spoons, and jars around the house. All you need are the opportunities to put them to good use.

Starting with pre-schoolers, use the assortment of cups and spoons that you have on hand. It's a way to familiarize children with these objects. The most common items to be measured will probably be sand and water. By all means, use the terminology of measurement as a way to familiarize the children with it: cup, pint, liter, quart, teaspoon, tablespoon, gallon. This will begin the understanding of these concepts for the children.

Once the children are school-aged, they can be helpful to you in the kitchen. Helping the parent who does the cooking is a great way to get involved in an activity that benefits the whole family. Asking for two cups of flour or three tablespoons of oil will involve the child in preparing food for the family, giving a sense of contribution in addition to concrete knowledge about measuring.

Another possible by-product of doing this work together can be the understanding of the concept that the role of the cook is not sex-specific: boys can do it as well as girls.

Linear measurement can also be a useful skill. Measuring boards or other items that have to be cut during home projects can lead to a greater understanding of this process. It gives children a better grasp of terms that are used in everyday speech: ten inches, one hundred feet, fifty yards, half a mile, ten miles, etc.

In so doing, you will also help your child to understand concepts of comparisons. Children can begin to comprehend, with your help, the meaning of *more*, *less*, and *equal* when they compare two items or quantities.

You also have an opportunity to use basic addition and subtraction skills by asking such questions as, "We have four cups of flour in the bowl. When we add two more, how many will we have all together?"

ESTIMATING

I like to do this activity in my classroom each October. When I suggest it to the parents of my students, they usually tell me that the family had a good time with it. So read this before you carve up your next Halloween pumpkin!

The pumpkin can help you to introduce a skill that can be improved only with practice: estimating.

When you've got all the insides scooped out, get that gloppy mass together and ask all the family members how many seeds they think there are. Perhaps one of the kids can serve as secretary for this one. (Make it a kid whose hands have not ventured into the pumpkin's guts!)

Chances are good that the younger the child, the higher the guess will be. Don't be surprised if your five-year-old guesses something like "a thousand," "a million," or "infinity." This indicates that he doesn't really understand the meaning of these numbers.

An exercise like this is valuable because it takes them closer to making numbers real for children. They have heard people talk about having fifty, one hundred, or one thousand of something, but do they actually understand what these figures mean? This is an opportunity to make a concrete relationship between a word for a number and the number itself.

After you count fifty or one hundred pumpkin seeds, give everyone a chance to revise his estimate. Emphasize that you are not in this to win anything; it's just family fun time. The older the child, the closer their estimates will be to reality.

During this process, ask an older child to explain her thinking to you. Or, if the kids are not able to verbalize theirs, share yours with them: "It looks like we have counted about half of the seeds," you explain. "So far there are 200. So, if that's about half, I think that there will be about 400 all together. 200 plus 200 equals 400."

Opportunities to estimate will present themselves in many ways: how many M & M's are in the bag? How many pennies are in a little jar? How many carrots are in the package? How many watermelon seeds are there? As you practice these activities with your children, you bring the reality of numbers to them.

PROBABILITY

When our Brian was just a little guy and wanted to know what the odds were that he would get what he wanted, he used to ask, "What are the percents?"

In other words, what were the chances that he would get what he wanted? 50-50? 60-40? 90-10? And which number was in his favor?

Information in the news is frequently reported in percentages. All those statistics and figures in the media will have no meaning until children can become accustomed to the way they are used.

Parent preparation can make this information meaningful and understandable to their children before they have the opportunity to use it in the classroom.

When I taught third and fifth grades, I found it helpful to use a tool that many children understood: the dollar. Once children know the units that make up a dollar (and especially that one hundred pennies is equivalent in value) they can relate percentages to that dollar.

In this way, they can begin to understand, for example, that a store having a sale of 10% off is not very enticing, yet 50% is a much better deal.

If children don't notice that the possible combinations of numbers always add up to 100, this is something you could point out: how one candidate has 40% of the electorate voting for her, one has 48%, and the remaining 12% is undecided.

Using and explaining the meaning of several familiar terms in our language can help to transmit the bigger picture to children.

When talking about voting, children can see that majority means at least one more than fifty percent.

Anyone giving 100 percent of effort is giving all of it.

Baseball fans have brought the term batting a thousand into the lexicon. (This is, of course, a misnomer since the "thousand" is really 1.000, with a decimal point instead of a comma.)

I'll bet that if you pay attention to percentages in your daily conversations with your child, she will have a better than 50-50 chance of understanding the concept when the topic is introduced in school.

CHAPTER 5:
SCIENCE

The important thing is not to stop questioning. Curiosity has its own reason for existing. One cannot help but be in awe when he contemplates the mysteries of eternity, of life, of the marvelous structures of reality. It is enough if one tries merely to comprehend a little of this mystery every day. Never lose a holy curiosity.

— Albert Einstein

SCIENCE IS EVERYWHERE

Historically, the United States has lagged behind many other nations in the instruction of science. With the increased use of technology in many people's daily lives, this has been changing.

Parents are in a position to encourage their children's interest in many different areas of science. Let your curiosity and that of your children lead you to the area that has the greatest interest to you.

Getting children to be curious about the natural world around them at an early age can lead them to science-related hobbies and jobs as they grow up. This is just a sampling of science-related activities for you and your family:

Animals (including people)

Watch a spider in its web; observe the movements of the animals around you: dogs, cats, squirrels, rabbits, birds; observe birds in their nests and their habitats; watch a caterpillar spin its cocoon and wait until it transforms into a butterfly; look for animal tracks; observe the way animals care for their young; visit the vet with your pet; observe the changes as a cut heals; ask to see x-rays at the doctor's or dentist's office; ask about the equipment that your doctor or dentist uses; observe the genetic similarities between generations in your family or friends.

Plants

Plant packaged seeds and observe them grow; plant seeds from fruit and vegetables that you eat; plant an acorn; learn the names of various types of trees and flowers; save waste food as compost; watch flowers bud and blossom; help care for trees and flowers in your environment; plant a tree and record its progress.

Weather

Look at the weather report on television or in the newspaper; pick a place and find its weather on the Internet; look at a map that has climate or weather zones; observe the sky at different times during the day; keep a thermometer inside and outside your house; fly a kite; ask people about the weather where they are when you send them e-mail or speak to them on the phone; keep a graph or diary of weather conditions; talk about the weather with people who come from different climate zones; investigate the life of people who live in a different weather zone than you; collect rain in a container; gaze at a rainbow; count the time that takes place after lightning flashes and thunder crashes; .

Chemical and physical properties

Experiment with what will sink or float in a large bucket of water; collect items in nature and sort them; see how long it takes for an ice cube to melt; draw on steamy bathroom mirrors or car windows; reflect light off mirrors; shine light through a crystal; balance objects on a seesaw; squirt food coloring into water; make bubbles; create your own musical instruments; sort spices by the different types of tastes; help with measuring and mixing with recipes; put glow-in-the-dark stickers on your child's ceiling or wall.

THE IMPORTANCE OF SCIENCE BOOKS FOR BOYS

Pat Cunningham, a teacher and author who gives workshops to other teachers around the country, made a fascinating point in her all-day seminar entitled *Teaching ALL Children to Read and Write*. She has noticed that many boys are much more interested in reading non-fiction than fiction. Therefore, if your son is a reluctant beginning reader, you may find that you can spark his interest in books much more easily if you provide non-fiction books. Books related to science topics are excellent for this purpose. Many boys love books about dinosaurs, trucks, the solar system, animals, the human body, volcanoes, and similar subjects.

VOCABULARY OF THE FIVE SENSES

Science awareness includes an extensive vocabulary concerning the body's five senses. Using a variety of words with your children helps to build vocabulary, which will be helpful when reading non-fiction books that are based on scientific fact.

There are many activities that can help children to become more aware of their five senses:

- Touch things while blindfolded. When I was in the Boy Scouts there was an evening when, sitting around a campfire, those of us who were on our first campout with the troop had to go through some rites of initiation. In one of them, we were blindfolded and had to put our hand into a can of "worms." They certainly felt like worms! They turned out to be pieces of cooked spaghetti in a small amount of water.

- Pinch the nose and taste something. The sense of taste is related to the sense of smell. Inability to smell what we are eating will affect its taste.

- Taste without looking. Put small amounts of food on the tongue of the child. See if she can tell by its taste and consistency what it is.

- Listen to the woods or other area at night. See what you can tell about what is there without seeing it.

- Look under a magnifying class or microscope. See what you can discover that can be seen without the naked eye.

Once children understand the abilities and vocabulary concerning their five senses, they can begin to understand the meaning behind such phrases as "sixth sense" and "extrasensory."

INCREASE YOUR VOCABULARY

Develop a knowledge about words associated with each of the five senses:

SIGHT/EYES			SMELL/NOSE	TASTE/TONGUE		
light	glossy	amplified	fruity	salty	dry	cool
dark	twinkle	bass	acrid	sweet	crispy	tepid
opaque	sparkle	treble	aroma	bitter	**TOUCH/SKIN**	rough
transparent	shimmer	twang	bouquet	sour	wet	texture
translucent	glow	sound waves	stink	spicy	dry	consistency
shadow		vibrations	fetid	smooth	smooth	fuzzy
shade	**HEARING/EARS**	tone	foul	crunchy	bumpy	scratchy
bright	clang	percussion	olfactory	minty	ridge	soft
shiny	high pitch	pitter-patter	fresh	fresh	hot	sharp
dull	low pitch		nostril	stale	cold	dull
matte	screech			juicy	warm	stiff
	muffled					limp

MADE IN NATURE OR BY PEOPLE?

Young children who are just coming to grips with how the world is put together enjoy figuring out and knowing where things come from. You can help with games that can solidify their sense of where things come from.

Made by nature or people?

Classify objects as to how they are made: were they made in nature or made by people? Many of the things around us use a combination of these. Your house, for example, has wood that was made in nature, but modified by people.

Children can understand that the physical properties of things can vary. They can be either solid, liquid, or gas. Water can be all three, turning from liquid to solid when it freezes and from liquid to gas when it boils and evaporates as steam.

Animal, vegetable, or mineral?

Everything your child sees can be classified as either an animal, vegetable, or mineral. In biology, there are two kingdoms: animal, of which we people are members, and plants. Matter from the earth — including rocks, dirt, and various metals — are minerals.

Help your child to analyze the characteristics of each of these categories. What do all animals have in common, if anything? What are the things that only certain animals have in common? How do the different families of animals differ from other families?

Are there similar features that are the same among all plants? Among all minerals? What are they?

WEATHER

Do your children notice the change in weather? You have several times during the year to point this out to them in order to give them an understanding of the change in seasons.

There are several observations that you can help your children make during this time of year: the decrease or increase in the amount of light per day, the cooler or warmer temperatures, the increasing or decreasing amount of rainfall, and the sprouting or falling of leaves.

The week before the change to Daylight Savings Time or Standard Time is a good time to make the relationship between when it is getting light and when it is getting dark. Why do we change the clocks in October and April? This makes a discussion of interest for children.

The number of days of sunshine may diminish as well. Make your own graph of the weather. In my classroom, we keep track of four types of weather: full sun, partial sun, full clouds, and rain. In some parts of the day, weather can change several times a day. If that is what it is like where you live, pick one time of day and chart the weather for that time. A convenient and constant time could be the time that everyone leaves the house to go to school.

At the end of the month, start a new chart for the next month. After you collect several months of these graphs, you can ask the children to make conclusions about the information that they have gathered: which month has the most sunny days? the most rainy days? How many days are there if you add the partially sunny and rainy days together?

Looking in the newspaper can give information about other parts of the country or the world. Many Sunday newspapers have weather charts with this information. Pick cities in which your children are interested and keep track of the differences between your area and that city. Perhaps it is where the kids' grandparents live, where they were born, or where you were born, where the family has visited, or where your children talk about visiting someday.

In addition to learning the fundamentals of science, your children can draw conclusions about the world around them.

CHANGING THE CLOCKS IN THE SPRING AND FALL

In the fall, we "fall back" and in the spring we "spring forward" one hour. Perhaps your child notices when it gets darker earlier or stays light longer, as well as gets a bit colder or warmer. This is a good time to talk about two issues: one scientific and one regarding home safety.

In a discussion about the changing number of hours of light and darkness, you will likely be talking about the earth's rotation on its axis, its revolving around the sun, the seasons, directions, the equinoxes (vernal and autumnal) and the solstices (summer and winter). It's a good way to get your child grounded in these concepts.

Ask the kids: What time is it now when it gets dark? Is it dark when you get up in the morning? Have them make note of the level of darkness, and then look at a clock. See how this compares to what they see on Sunday morning and evening, after the time has been changed.

Many newspapers and almanacs print the time of sunrise and sunset. On the Internet you could Ask Jeeves (www.ask.com) for the time at many given locations. Over the next few months, keep track of the changing times. For older kids, see how the number of hours of light changes until the winter solstice, then reverses.

The International Association of Fire Chiefs, along with a battery company, promotes a home safety fire awareness program coincident with the changing of our clocks from Daylight Savings Time. They use this as a reminder to check the batteries in your home smoke alarms.

Their brochure tells us that 92% of all American homes have smoke alarms. One third of these alarms do not work, however, because the battery is either worn out or missing. They say that the chances of surviving a home fire nearly doubles when an effective smoke alarm is in your home.

The time, then, is right for these two lessons: learning about the earth's rotation and keeping your family safer in the event of a home fire. Please don't keep your kids in the dark about either issue.

FAMILIES IN NATURE

When I brought lily bulbs to my class for planting in pots, our study took a turn I hadn't quite anticipated. (Maybe you've noticed that this happens a lot with kids!)

I expected to talk about the needs of plants and what the flowers would look like as they grew. We did that. But before we got into that, I had the bulbs in a metal tray, the children gathered around, and I asked them, What are these?

Nobody knew that they were lily bulbs, but lots of kids thought that they were onions. This made me recall my own surprise when I had learned, many years ago, that the lily and onion are members of the same botanical family.

"How can the onion and lily be in the same family?" the kids wanted to know. We talked about family characteristics and tried to relate the topic to things that are similar among people in their own families.

In order to get the point across in a broader way, we talked about the way other types of animals have similar features: wolves, dogs, and coyotes have similarities amongst themselves the way cougars, cats, lions, and tigers do. Mice, rats, hamsters, and guinea pigs have similarities. These are observations that most of the kids had already made. We got into the characteristics that are shared by all mammals, and some kids expressed surprise that whales were mammals and not fish.

The kids enjoyed looking for similarities among other groups of animals. Some were motivated to learn terms that cover several related animals, such as *primates, marsupials, reptiles, felines, canines.*

This led to other words that, while not referring to families of animals or plants, do refer to characteristics that are shared by groups of animals: *carnivores, herbivores, omnivores, warm-blooded, cold-blooded, nocturnal, diurnal.*

Children are looking for ways to make sense in their world. Pointing out these similarities and putting groups of animals or plants in the same family for children or finding other ways to group them is a sorting process that helps them to come to this understanding.

HOW THINGS WORK

How does a computer work? How does a car run? How does water get into our house? How does stuff flow to the bay from the storm drain?

You have kids. Kids have questions. There is no separating the two. Kids are curious about the world. Some parents are lucky: they have a good grip on the way things work, and they are able to explain these workings to children. From the motor of a refrigerator to the inner gears of a clock, you can satisfy your child's need to have answers. But not all parents can do this.

It's humbling, but it needs to be done occasionally: you have to tell your child that you do not know the answer to her questions. What you do in these situations can be formative in her education.

A "let's find out" attitude on the part of a parent teaches a variety of lessons to your child. First of all, your child learns that there are places to look for answers to questions: the library, the Internet, the local science museum, or another person who has a greater knowledge base than you.

Secondly, she begins to understand the different means necessary for getting the answers. More and more, the computer is coming into play, whether people use the Internet or search the now-computerized card catalog at the library. Each medium works differently and needs a different skill set for finding answers.

Thirdly, children get an understanding that adults are not omnipotent. And, hey, if adults don't know everything, it's okay that they, children, don't have to know everything, too!

Learning does not end at the completion of the formal education process. This attitude puts children in a good position to see learning as a lifelong activity. Children learn this when they see adults help them to find answers to their questions.

Maybe that's why college graduation is usually called commencement. Think of it as the beginning — not the end — of learning.

BOOKS THAT SHOW HOW

David Macaulay has written many books that show the inner workings and behind-the-scenes of a variety of topics. *The New Way Things Work* is a 1998 revision of his earlier work, *The Way Things Work*. He has also written and illustrated a dazzling array of books that give detailed looks at the construction of many objects (titles include *Cathedral, Castle, Mill, Pyramid, Ship, City,* and *Underground*). Each tome contains narratives, diagrams, cut-aways, and explanation of the building process. Any child who is mechanically minded will enjoy one or all of these books.

TECHNOLOGY

The pace of technological advancements has accelerated in recent years, and there is no sign that it will slow. If anything, we can expect that today's elementary school children will have increased involvement with technology as they advance through school and head into the workforce.

The range of machinery outside of school is significantly greater than that inside. Therefore, it is parents whose facility with technology will pave the way for their children's comfort in this arena. What can you do?

- Point out and explain the machines that you use in your family's life. There is bound to be a tremendous variety: telephone, computer, car, television, VCR, thermostat, clock, and radio are just a few.

- Let them explore machines. If you have a broken appliance, hand it over to the kids, along with an assortment of screwdrivers and other tools. Giving them an opportunity to take apart and experiment with the variety of pieces in your household appliances will help them to make an approach in much the way scientists begin their own experiments.

- You can share the same understanding in person with your child as you take the time together to examine the construction of a new home in your neighborhood or of a building project in your own home.

An important concept that your child can learn is that construction must be accomplished in a pre-defined number of steps. Each step builds on a previous one.

It is the hands-on work that gets children fired-up about science and technology. Give them a chance to find out, "How does this work?," "What's under this?," and wonder, "What would happen if...."

PLANTS

If you do not have an outdoor place in which to plant seeds, indoor flower pots will do. This is an activity that is easy to work on together at home and it can be a fun lesson for children to learn about the way things grow.

You may buy seeds, but you can also sprout several things that you probably already have in the house: a potato, sweet potato, or carrot top are three items that many people already have on hand. Or you could see what happens when you plant seeds from fruit or vegetables you eat at home.

The Tiny Seed is a wonderful book by Eric Carle. It chronicles the cycle of a seed being planted and growing into a flower. This is but one of many cycles of life that children can learn about in order to appreciate the wonder of the world around them.

Another Eric Carle book, *Pancakes, Pancakes*, follows the steps it takes to be able to put pancakes on the breakfast table — from harvesting wheat to making the pancakes. It is a great example for showing children that what they eat had a beginning in nature and didn't just pop out of a box purchased in the grocery store.

Many other books explain the benefits of plants to people. I have found that children as young as first graders can understand the process through which plants take in carbon dioxide and give out oxygen, while people do the opposite. This is an example through which we explain to children the relationship that people have with plants, and how important they are to us.

Planting seeds and watching them grow puts children in touch with a vital force of nature. It is an easy way to give them this connection, and leads to a respect and understanding of the process on which we all depend for food and oxygen.

HAPPY EARTH DAY TO YOU!

By getting our children involved in Earth-friendly practices when they are young, we have a better chance in making sure that these activities will become second nature as they grow up.

Children of all ages can contribute to the family, the neighborhood, the community, and the Earth. Here are but a few approaches that families can take to make their children aware of their need to be part of solutions to environmental concerns that we have:

An activity that is easy to practice at home is sorting recyclable materials. This process is an important skill that is a precursor to learning how to read and write!

Youngsters' imaginations can invent new uses for otherwise used-up containers and boxes. What kinds of games can they create? Empty boxes and other containers can be kept from going into landfill if they become part of your children's play activities.

As school-aged children tire of their toys, games, books, and other possessions, perhaps they can make arrangements with friends and classmates to trade objects among themselves. In so doing, they learn how to keep these items from making their way to landfill. Perhaps more importantly, they can learn that they do not have to rely on new and/or expensive items for satisfaction.

Children have a natural affinity for animals. It is in this area that they can find many activities to encourage the proliferation of the fauna in their environment: making a bird feeder or birdbath is simple. Flowers can be planted to attract butterflies and hummingbirds. Many zoo programs have programs through which people can "adopt" animals to help in their care.

Most important in this area is our attitude in working with children on the things that all of us can do to improve our environment. It is our responsibility to lead them to understand that our actions are part of a larger cooperative effort that can make a difference.

AN EARTH DAY BOOK TO USE ALL YEAR

My favorite children's book on this topic is written to help them understand how they fit into the complex cycle of nature. It is *50 Simple Things Kids Can Do to Save the Earth.*

RECYCLING CRAYONS

There is a second chance for all those old crayons you have! LAF Lines, Ltd. will take your old crayons and process them into new ones, made completely from old and broken recycled crayons. This can be done as a family project for your own little ones or as a group project involving your child's class, school, scout troop, or neighborhood. For details, contact them at 1-800-561-0922.

REDUCE, REUSE, RECYCLE

The third week in October has been promoted since 1997 as Second Chance Week in California. This is a fine time, just six months from Earth Day, to remind our young people about some basic principles that apply all year long. The principles involved are applicable whether you live in California or not.

The watchwords of Second Chance Week are, "Resell, reuse, and repair. Give it a second chance." The promoters cite a compelling bit of information from the first Second Chance Week, held just two years ago: in 1997, their efforts helped in the reuse of 90 tons of used goods and materials statewide; last year it increased to 100 tons.

If you studied chemistry you may remember the principle of the conservation of matter: matter is neither created nor destroyed in any of its changes. This is an important consideration as people throw away items that they no longer need. This stuff ends any possibility of having a useful life, then goes to a landfill.

The parents' mission, then, is to help their progeny find ways to prolong the time until the unwanted items from become part of a landfill.

Most kids own several things they no longer use. Consider with them these possibilities:

- Find things they don't want and give them to somebody else: siblings, neighbors, cousins, classmates, and friends are good candidates.

- Arrange a swap meet under parental supervision with a bunch of friends. Everyone brings items no longer needed and exchanges these for ones they can use.

- Find organizations that can use their old things. When considering recipients, don't forget your current or former teachers!

- Have a garage sale.

- Put together a creative and one-of-a-kind Halloween outfit without spending any money for a new costume that will be worn only once and then hidden away or discarded. A scarf, string of beads, funny necktie, or an oversized garment from a parent or older sibling, along with some props, can fill the bill.

For more information about Second Chance Week, you can go to the website at www.choose2reuse.org or call toll-free at 888-385-7240.

CHAPTER 6:
SOCIAL STUDIES

You've got to be taught to be afraid

Of people whose eyes are oddly made

And people whose skin is a different shade.

You've got to be carefully taught.

DIVERSITY IN PEOPLE

The word *social* in *social studies* refers to people; that is the focus of social studies — people: their history, where they come from, how they live, and what they celebrate. We live in a pluralistic society, a beautiful mosaic that would look quite different if all the tiles were the same color.

Our nation is rich with its diversity of people. Children who accept these differences at an early age will have an easier time as they come into contact with different others during their school years.

One of the most familiar areas in which children can appreciate the abundance of variety in their lives is food. Whether you dine in restaurants or at home, lead your children to the understanding that their food choices have been greatly enhanced, thanks to the sharing of cuisines from other cultures. Chances are your children have favorite foods that span several continents. Help them to notice this.

I hope your family has a regular schedule in which you return and check out batches of library books. If you don't have that yet, try to work it into your routine. A child's choice of books is a tremendous motivation toward improvement of reading. Be sure to choose a few books yourself, though, to fill in the gaps. Books about other cultures, either folk tales or non-fiction, are a tremendously underused section in many libraries.

Perhaps your child overhears a news report about a foreign country while you are watching the news. See if you can find a book about that country on the next visit to the library.

You'd be surprised how people show their own cultural biases in their speech. I have frequently heard Americans talk about how the British drive on the *wrong* side of the road. A person who is being sensitive and open to other cultures would say that they drive on the *opposite* side of the road. They aren't *wrong* for doing this — just *different*.

Teachers incorporate partner and group activities into class work. Children need to be able to focus on the task at hand in such a way that the physical or cultural differences of other people will not detract from the assignment. Your preparation at home can be a big help.

You've got to be taught

Before it's too late,

Before you are six or

seven or eight,

To hate all the people your

relatives hate.

You've got to be carefully

taught.

— Oscar Hammerstein
"Carefully Taught" from
South Pacific

85

YOU'RE A CULTURAL ANTHROPOLOGIST!

The other day I noticed this legend on a t-shirt: "Only nepotism will get you a better job." It advertised a website through which people can find jobs. It got me to thinking: What could a foreigner — either from another country, another planet, or traveling from another time period — learn about us, based on what he sees on t-shirts that people are wearing?

Cultural anthropologists study living cultures and people. You and your child can use their method called participant observation without ever traveling to a foreign destination. This is how they understand cultures and how those cultures adapt and contribute to both local and global history, economy, politics, and social changes.

Together, you and your child can pick an item that you would like to observe, and see what you can find out by looking at it. Let's say you continue with my t-shirt example. You'll look to see what you can find out about people by what is written on their t-shirts.

Write down what you see. Depending on the age of your child, you can take turns being the scribe. After you have collected your data, it is time to analyze it. What kinds of messages have you observed?

Find a way to categorize what you saw. You may find that one category is schools (from elementary to university), one is sports teams, one is cities or countries, one is advertising. See what you come up with.

Several skills are enhanced by doing this, including writing, reading, drawing conclusions, and sharpening powers of observation. There is also the added benefit of working together between parent and child(ren), which is terrific for oral language development.

What are some other things that you can observe this way? How about billboards, bumper stickers, and hats?

If you travel, you can make observations about any one of a number of things: the way houses look in the area you are visiting, the types of cars you see on the road, the kind of clothing people wear, the types of stores where people shop, the kinds of bread or other food that they eat, etc.

IF YOU CAN'T TRAVEL, LOOK AT BOOKS

There is an abundance of books about different cultures that have been published in the last ten years. Children enjoy learning about the cultures of other people. You can enhance your child's learning by exposing her to as many of these as possible. If your child knows family members, neighbors, or classmates from other countries, these books are an excellent source of information that can supplement what you find out from the people your child has met.

TIME CAPSULE

By assembling personal mementos, family members can act as cultural anthropologists, preserving artifacts for "discovery" during a later time.

Putting together a time capsule for each of your children can also further their understanding of history and writing. Most time capsules are buried, which means that consideration needs to be paid to deterioration of items placed in the ground. This project needn't necessarily take that approach.

Your child's time capsule can be placed in a sealed box and put away in a closet or other out-of-the-way place. Limit the items by defining the container in which they will be placed. You probably have a shoe box around; if not, save one from the next pair of shoes you buy.

Help your child to decide what the contents of the time capsule will define: a year in his life, a summer of activities, a family trip, etc. You may have lots of souvenirs from a vacation, so that is a fine place to start. Then you can go ahead and help to gather the items that have significance for the time period you have chosen.

Here is a list to use as a jumping-off point for the items you may place into the box: photos, post cards, maps, journal, newspaper, magazine articles, pictures of heroes and heroines, video, toys, collection cards (baseball, Pokémon), coins or bills from foreign travel, letters from family members, birthday cards, school creative writing or research assignment, report card, a favorite book, an article of clothing.

Children who are not able to write on their own can dictate stories to older children or adults who, in turn, can write them out by hand or on a computer. A family time capsule can include something written by each member of the family.

Make an agreement among yourselves as to when the capsule will be opened and viewed by the family members. You may even decide that this is a project that can be assembled annually, for retrieval in ten years or so.

87

GEOGRAPHY

The question I ask my first-graders sounds easy enough: "What state do we live in?" The most popular answer: "The United States." I can see I have my work cut out for me, geographically speaking.

I shouldn't be too surprised, as this reflects the national disgrace that most Americans are pitifully ignorant about geography. Parents can help bring greater geographic and global awareness to their children. Here are a few family activities. All you need is an atlas or globe as a reference tool:

- When you shop for groceries, look for labels on fruit, vegetables, and other food items to indicate the country or region of origin.

- Look on the labels in your family's clothing and other household items.

- If your family speaks another language besides English, talk to your child about its country of origin. When you hear people speaking other languages, teach your child to be respectful of this. Most people, if approached in a friendly way, will be delighted to teach you and your child a few words of their native tongue.

- Plant nurseries are full of greenery that originates from many places around the world. Public gardens usually label their growth so that you can find out about areas of origin. If you don't find labels, ask around for a docent or brochure.

- Whether your favorite source for news is television, newspaper, radio, or the Internet, the media is rich with references to other countries.

- Use direction words such as north, south, east, and west to describe where you are walking or driving. Relate these words to the directions used on maps. The same principles are involved whether you are using a road map or atlas.

- When communicating with family members who live outside your immediate area, talk with the children about the city, state, or country in which they live.

- Take a walk around the world in an atlas. Even if you have an old one — one that still has divisions such as East and West Germany — you can still use that as a lesson to teach your child that these used to be different countries but now they have been re-joined.

- When your child shows deeper interest, move from the atlas to books that cover history, language, and customs of other peoples. In so doing, you will have a child who is well prepared for geographic references wherever she encounters them.

GEOGRAPHY THROUGH MUSIC

One day, we were grooving to the oldies on the car radio when Neil Diamond came on: "Kentucky woman, she shines with her own kind of light."

"What's a Kentucky woman?" our then-seven-year-old Elizabeth wanted to know. Ah, thought I, recognizing a teachable moment when I saw one. And we launched into a geography lesson, discussing states and cities around the U.S.

When she was six years old, Elizabeth enjoyed singing "Meet Me in St. Louis" from the movie of the same name. We used the opportunity to take out an atlas and sing our way around the map.

How many songs with geographical locations come through your home or car radio every day? What are your family favorites? "Deep in the Heart of Texas," "New York, New York," and "California Dreamin'" reflect some of our family history and interests. Ricky Nelson's "Traveling Man" takes a trip around the world, with more than enough exploring to cover a session with an atlas.

There are several advantages of working with your child in this fashion. It enhances her knowledge of geography, you get to share your love of music, and, most of all, it's a terrific way to spend time together.

TRAVELING MUSIC

Here are some song titles that include geographic references. How many more can you and yoru family find? There must be hundreds!

"Allentown"	"California, Here I Come"	"Carry Me Back to Old Virginia"
"America"	"Chattanooga Choo-Choo"	"Ferry Cross the Mersey"
"Blue Hawaii"	"The Erie Canal"	"Fifty Nifty United States"
"Chicago"	"Moonlight in Vermont"	"Midnight Train to Georgia"
"Big 'D'"	"The Tennessee Waltz"	"Rhode Island is Famous for You"
"Oh, Shenandoah"	"The Yellow Rose of Texas"	
"Oklahoma!"	"The Atcheson, Topeka, and Santa Fe"	"When the Midnight Choo Choo Leaves for Alabam'"
"San Francisco"		

WHOSE NAME IS THAT?

Children can gain an understanding of their local history and a sense of connection to it if they learn the origins of local names on such places as schools, streets, parks, and other topographical features.

Some names — Washington, Lincoln, Hoover, Mark Twain — are well-known Americans who made worthy contributions to our society. Telling our children about these people will give them an appreciation and understanding of why streets and schools were named after them.

People of other origins are represented with such names as Cowper (England), Pasteur (France), and Portola (Spain). It is likely that children will run into these names outside of our area.

National and international names such as these are common in every part of our country. Our lifetimes have seen a trend in which we can now find the same names on restaurants and stores from one end of our land to another. These are no longer markers that distinguish one place from another.

What, then, does make any one town different from another nowadays? Part of this distinction can be found in local names.

We use geographic identifiers in our speech almost every day with the names of our schools, streets, parks and nearby landmarks. Each of these names, and many more, come from people who were early settlers of an area.

Local connections are abundant in every community. Your historical association is a resource for tracing names to the early times of the founding of our community.

The skill of tracking down the namesake for a local point of interest will serve your child well in her education. It won't be too long before she will be doing much more rigorous research than that! Start her off early with the answers to local questions and watch her gain confidence as she eventually explores the rest of the world with the same thirst for knowledge.

THE MEANINGS OF HOLIDAYS:
DR. MARTIN LUTHER KING, JR.

When schools, government agencies, and businesses are closed in honor of Dr. Martin Luther King, Jr., do your children understand why?

Talking about the meaning of a holiday can give children a deeper understanding and appreciation of its importance — not only in the history of our country, but in our own lives as individuals.

One of the more striking aspects between this holiday and one such as Presidents' Day, celebrated the following month, is that many of today's parents were alive during the time that Dr. King lived.

Secondly, there are film and videotape of him speaking. Though some of the scenes may be dated by now, the people don't look that much different than they do today.

Most importantly, we can remember changes in our lives that have been made as a result of the work that Dr. King and many other people have done.

In a very real sense, we are a link to this recent history because we can recall specifics about this historical figure and the times in which he lived. This distinguishes our talk about him and his ideals from those of such people as Washington and Lincoln. It doesn't make the older presidents' lives and contributions less significant — it just removes us from them because none of us, or anyone we know, was alive during their times.

Were you active in the Civil Rights Movement? Did you live in or ever visit a place where segregation was the norm? Did you hear any of Dr. King's speeches or sermons in person? Do you remember where you were when you heard the news that he had been shot? What did you experience in the days following his death? What changes have you made in your own perspective since those days?

The impressions that you convey to your child will help to bring history closer to her.

To follow up and get more information with your youngster, visit the website at www.stanford.edu/group/King, which includes many of Dr. King's papers, speeches, and sermons.

A STORY FOR EACH DAY

Talk with your child about the significance of these holidays: Presidents' Day, Memorial Day, Independence Day, Labor Day, and Thanksgiving. Religious holidays, too, are steeped in tradition. There are also many holidays celebrated locally that are not national in scope. If your area celebrates one of these, talk to your child about it.

BLACK HISTORY MONTH

February is Black History Month. This is an opportunity for you to help your child understand the contributions and accomplishments that African-Americans have made to our society and the world.

Appreciating any one group of people begins with the story of any one person. You know your child well enough to understand where his interests lie. As we look at the achievements of African-Americans, you have a diversity of people from whom to choose: activists, artists, athletes, leaders, business entrepreneurs, musicians, educators, inventors, scientists, and explorers.

Every cultural group in our society has had its triumphs as well as its struggles. If we can help children to identify with the triumphs and struggles of any one person, they can relate more successfully to other people — either of that same culture, their own, or any other.

For that reason, I like the approach of exposing children to the biographies and autobiographies of people whose lives can teach them about the humanity that we share across any kind of cultural or racial divide.

If your child is an athlete, he may appreciate the story of Jackie Robinson or Michael Jordan. A child who likes stories about explorers may appreciate a book about Matthew Henson or Mae Jemison. The child who enjoys performing may identify with the story of Marian Anderson or Whitney Houston. The scientist in your family would do well to emulate George Washington Carver or Dr. Charles R. Drew.

There is a fine assortment of story books written by such prolific children's authors as Donald Crews, Faith Ringgold, Patricia McKissack, and Jerry Pinkney.

The most important aspect of this is the understanding that we live in a society that has been created by people from many different backgrounds. It is necessary to respect and understand those who are culturally different from us.

Celebrating the achievements of others puts us in a frame of mind to want to make positive contributions ourselves to the society in which we live.

WOMEN'S HISTORY MONTH

"Every time a girl reads a womanless history, she learns she is worth less." - Myra and David Sadker in *Failing at Fairness: How America's Schools Cheat Girls*.

March is National Women's History Month. "Why do we have a Women's History Month and not a Men's History Month?" asked one of my first-graders, a six-year-old boy. The question is fair enough — and food for thought.

Academic reviews have shown that most United States history books in our country have less than 11% of their content that deals with women. As a result of this, students - boys and girls alike - can understandably draw the conclusion that women have been passive and non-participatory throughout history.

With that in mind, in 1978 Women's History Week was begun by a group of educators in Sonoma County, California. By 1987, Congress declared a resolution making March National Women's History Month. A declaration was signed by President Reagan.

Since then, the history of women in our society has been moved to a place where it has not been before: as in integral part of the school curriculum and in the forefront of the minds of many more people.

We have quite a way to go if we are looking for parity on the national level. Women are 52% of our population; that should be reflected in our Congress. In 1999, of the 100 Senators, only nine were women. (In California and Maine, *both* Senators at the time were women.) Of the 435 members of the House of Representatives, only 56 (13%) were women.

Who are the women who most influenced you? It would be valuable to both sons and daughters to talk about these women — whether they were famous or not — and their character traits that affected your life.

In conclusion, I propose a corollary to the Sadkers' opening quotation: Every time a boy reads a womanless history, he learns that women are worth less. Don't we want both our girls and our boys to value women and their place in our society?

VOTING

Presidential elections happen only every four years, but many communities have elections for something or other every year, and sometimes twice a year.

Your child's early awareness of the process of elections can help to guide him to become an informed voter when he grows up. There is much that parents can do to make their children aware of the process of voting:

- If you display a sign in front of your house or a bumper sticker on your car, you probably feel passionate about a candidate or issue. Talk to your child about your choice. Keep the concepts appropriate to their ages, but do talk about it.

- Follow newspaper articles about your candidates and issues.

- Watch televised campaign speeches and the conventions.

- Talk about how the issues that the candidates are talking about affect you, your family, and your community.

- In the case of ballot initiatives, explain both sides of these issues.

- Help your child to read the signs and bumper stickers that you see when you are out together. Recognizing the symbols and characteristics of printed literature is an excellent skill that correlates to learning how to read.

- When the campaign literature arrives in the mail, go over it with your child.

- If you get an absentee ballot, show your child how it works. You can also show your child how you use it. If you feel that your vote is private and to be kept to yourself, by all means tell that to your child.

- Talk about the various offices for which you vote. Familiarize your child with the meaning of the terminology: city councilman/woman, alderman/woman, mayor, supervisor, assemblyman/woman, state senator, United States senator, representative, governor, vice president, president. If you don't explain these jobs to your child, she may not know what they mean.

Being an informed voter is a civic responsibility for all adults. Taking it seriously is one way to set an example to your child.

CHAPTER 7:
CREATIVE EXPRESSION

THE IMPORTANCE OF THE ARTS

In my years in the classroom, I have had the pleasure of teaching several children who have either one or two artists as parents. These children, who have a higher than average exposure to art and the media for creating it, possess some qualities that many other children do not have: in addition to their artistic talent, I have observed that they usually read and write better than their peers. My conclusion, based solely on this anecdotal evidence, is that their exposure to art affects other aspects of their learning.

This led me to a discussion with Aiko Cuneo, an artist who works with children in public schools, to flesh out the benefits of arts education, both in and out of schools. We offer to you these highlights of our conversation.

- First of all, we suggest that parents expand their definition of art. If you are a baker or a cook, if you like to arrange flowers, if you enjoy the harmonious arrangement of objects in your home, you are an artist. These expressions of creativity are as legitimate and valuable as those of painters and the other people called artists.

- If you are a scientist and enjoy inventing and experimenting, you bring an artistic sensibility to your work and may include yourself in the definition of artist.

- The role of parents and teachers is to expose children to a variety of materials so that they can create art. Once the variety is offered, children will then have a choice as to whether they want to use the materials or not. But without the exposure, there is no choice.

- Budding artists have a creative spirit that cannot be expressed unless there is an exposure to art. If you start early, there is a greater opportunity for this spirit to be identified and, therefore, grow with the child.

- Art is a delightful way through which you can record the development of your child's growth. Just as you will notice that writing and reading improves with age, so does artwork. Notice the difference between a self-portrait as drawn by a kindergartner compared to the same child's work as a third-grader.

It is the openness and awareness and innocence of sorts that I try to cultivate in my dancers. Although, as the Latin verb to educate, educare, indicates, it is not a question of putting something in but drawing it out, if it is there to begin with... I want all of my students and all of my dancers to be aware of the poignancy of life at that moment. I would like to feel that I had, in some way, given them the gift of themselves.

— Martha Graham

- Creating art is a fine way for children to make choices and solve problems. Every step involves making a decision: what color to use, how to make a line, what size to make something. With every choice the object becomes more and more their own.

- Everyone has an imagination. Art takes it a step further. Through art, children create something that, until that point, was only imagined. Thus, they create visual manifestations of abstract ideas.

- Children who may be having difficulties in other parts of the school curriculum may find an expressive outlet through art. It's a way to uncover talent that may not be seen otherwise.

- Art is a means of communicating ideas, feelings, and solutions in a way other than verbally or written.

In a ten-year national study by Shirley Brice Heath of Stanford University, it was discovered that young people who are involved in highly effective nonschool arts-based community programs in under-resourced communities, in comparison with a national sample of students were:

- four times more likely to win an academic award, such as being on the honor roll.

- eight times more likely to receive a community service award.

- three times more likely to win a school attendance award.

- four times more likely to participate in a math or science fair.

- likely to score higher on their SAT college admission test scores if they have been involved for more than four years of after-school arts study.

CREATING YOUR OWN ART STUDIO AT HOME

Put together an "art studio" in your home. Stock it with a variety of tools and materials: crayons, markers, pencils, stapler, fingerpaints, children's scissors, pastels, watercolors, brushes, glues or glue stick, clay, playdough, polymer clay, yarn, tape, beads, shells, empty rolls from toilet paper and paper towels, papers of various sizes and textures, wallpaper scraps, old maps, wrapping paper, intriguing found objects, leftovers from your own home improvement, boxes and containers of all sizes.

It is typical that those who fund school programs have seen the visual and performing arts as frills — programs that can be added only when there is enough money for them, as well as the first to be cut if there is a budget crisis.

Families can create a harmonious balance in their children's lives when they make provisions for the arts. Following are ideas to incorporate them into your home life.

- When you read to your children, be dramatic. Act out stories with props and costumes. Encourage them to create their own stories to act out for you.

- Save old Halloween costumes for dress-up fun. Add to the collection with clothing you no longer need: hats, scarves, purses, shoes, and items you can find inexpensively at garage sales.

- Expand your musical repertoire at home and in the car. Venture into unknown musical territory so that you and the children can hear something out of your usual fare. This can be easily expanded by turning to different radio stations and by checking out cassettes and CDs from the public library — all for free!

- While the music is playing at home, dance together. Teach your children traditional dances you know or improvise with them. Body movement is fun and good exercise.

- Sing together. Teach the kids your favorite songs. Many of them allow for verses that can be made up and have an endless and hilarious number of rhymes added to it.

- Look for arts programs after school, on weekends, and during vacations. Many community park and recreation departments offer these. Summer camps based on the arts are a good departure from the typical competitive sports camps.

- Create a scrapbook together. Put photos, memorabilia, drawings, and captions together creatively. In doing so, you will not only have a shared experience but a memory that will last for many years (if you use acid-free paper).

The most important ingredient in the recipe is your interest. Be there to appreciate and encourage during every step of the creative process.

DISPLAYING YOUR CHILD'S ART

"Hang it up in the living room, Mommy," your child suggests when she brings home her latest masterpiece from school or day care.

You know it doesn't go with the decor, but what do you do with the incoming flood of art that your little Picasso or Mary Cassatt brings home?

A child's artwork is an expression of his joy. Children — especially younger children — do not usually spend a lot of time planning artwork. These pieces are spontaneous and lively. The art is generally an accurate picture of what is going on in the child's mind. For this reason, children have some emotional attachment to the work because it is an expression of their sense of self. By extension, your acceptance and enthusiasm about the art is interpreted as acceptance and enthusiasm about the child herself.

My years in the classroom have taught me a crucial thing about the process of talking with children about their art. I have learned not to assume that I know what the subject is. Too many times have I remarked by saying something like, "I really like this picture of your dog playing in the field," only to hear something like, "That's Godzilla attacking the planet Neldor."

For that reason, my approach to looking at children's art is a lot more general. I might say something like, Thanks for showing this to me. Tell me about it. And then I listen, which provides me with information to use for other questions.

Adults can also say many other things to show that we are paying attention to the art — and, in turn, to the child. Think about statements such as these: You really have a good eye for color. I love the way this blue swirls into the green. You sure are learning a lot about using watercolors. What a field of flowers! Looking at the rainbow you made makes me feel happy.

And then, of course, you show your appreciation by finding a good place to display the work so your family and visitors can enjoy it with you.

ART MUSEUMS AND GALLERIES

Art nourishes the soul. It feeds us in a way that academics do not.

Children should experience art so that they can appreciate what is possible in the creative minds, as well as seeing the diversity of responses to the world around us.

Museums are repositories of treasures that can be thousands of years old. I remember being a fourth-grader and visiting the Egyptian exhibits in one of the finest museums in the world, the Metropolitan Museum of Art. In many collections, there is something for just about every taste: clothing, jewelry, household items, weapons, paintings, sculpture, toys, and small-scale models.

Art galleries are open at no charge for people to come in and take a look. When you are downtown, stop in for a few minutes to share what is there with your child.

Before you do this, talk about the no-touching policy. Children are very tactile and will otherwise want to experience the art with their fingers. The gallery owners will appreciate your taking care of this beforehand!

Exhibits can open a dialogue between parent and child about what they see, what they think, and what they feel when they view the works.

FINGER-PAINT

1 cup of corn starch or laundry starch

Enough cold water to make a smooth, thin paste

1 cup soap flakes

1/2 cup salt

1 quart water

1 teaspoon glycerin

Add the corn starch or laundry starch with enough cold water to make a smooth, thin paste. Add the soap flakes and salt. Put this in the top of a double boiler and add the water. Cook until it is thick. Beat with an egg beater. Add the glycerin to make it more pliable and gentler on the hands.

A quicker no-cook method (that may not last as long) can be made by adding dry tempera paint to liquid starch.

RECIPES FOR FUN

When was the last time you got your hands wet with finger paint and rubbed them all over paper? This activity was a favorite of mine in my childhood days.

The entire family can share the creative process: mixing the paint, preparing the area where you will play, creating the art, cleaning up, and deciding where and how to display or otherwise use the finished products.

Perhaps you will prefer ready-made paint. But if you would like the added activity of having your children read or listen to directions, at left is a recipe for making some of your own.

Have the kids spread out newspapers to protect the area where you will be creating your art. A good cover-up to keep clothes (relatively) clean is a large t-shirt; I use these in my classroom rather than old dress shirts, as they are easier for kids to put on and take off by themselves.

Kids can create their art on plain paper. Finger paint paper is available at many art supply stores. One possibility for the finished products is to display them intact around your home. Alternatively, you can cut up the large sheets to add an artistic touch to plain note cards — either home-made or store-bought — by affixing them on the front.

In this way, you can share small samples of your family's art with people to whom you write. It's also a fine way to have the kids write a few words to their grandparents, cousins, and other loved ones when you send out notes.

PLAYDOUGH

3 cups flour

3 teaspoons cream of tartar

3 cups cold water

1 1/2 cups salt

6 teaspoons oil

a few drops of food coloring

Stir all ingredients together. (You can get a lump-free consistency by using an electric beater or mixer.) Cook over a low heat for eight to ten minutes. Turn over while cooking.

Knead on foil paper. Add food coloring and knead until even, to pie crust consistency. Optional: if you would like to add a fragrance to the playdough, use sugar-free Kool-Aid.

PART 2: VALUES

The important thing is not so much that every child should be taught, as that every child should be given the wish to learn.

— John Lubbock

CHAPTER 8:
SHAPING ATTITUDES

Teach them it is better to shoot for the stars and miss than to aim for a pile of manure and hit it.

— Bob Algozzine

OPEN-ENDED QUESTIONS

Wouldn't you like to know what is going on in your child's mind? Isn't it amazing to see the thinking process at work? One of the joys of being around children is seeing how they work to make sense of their world. Tapping into this process is eye-opening to parents and teachers alike.

One way to get closer to your child's thought process is by asking open-ended questions. This type of question is a way to encourage her to use her existing knowledge and intertwine it with conjecture.

An open-ended question is one for which there is not only one answer. This also means that there is neither a correct or incorrect response.

When you talk to your child, you never know where the conversation will lead when you use open-ended questions. Imagine being together in a new setting and asking, "What does this remind you of?" There is something that reminds you of one place, but there is very likely something about it that recalls a totally different experience to your child

In a situation where events have not gone well, you can encourage your child to think through an alternative action by asking, "What could you do differently the next time?"

Even the very youngest of children can explain what they are up to if you ask, during the process of making something creative, "What do you call those things you're using?"

When children know something that I wouldn't expect them to know, I ask, "How do you know?" That's a good way to check where the knowledge came from or to see if the kid is making something up.

Here are some more open-ended questions and examples of how you may want to ask them with your young ones:

- When they are constructing something, ask, "Is there anything else you could use?"

- At a turning point in a story you are reading, ask, "What do you think will happen next?"

- When a character gets himself in a jam, ask, "What would you do if you were in that situation?"

- When she tells you the answer to a math problem, ask, "How did you figure that out?"

- When you are talking about a book you read or a movie you saw together, ask, "What would you have done differently?" and "Why?"

Asking questions is also a way to promote the values that you hold dear. Because there are many ways to answer, you can get insight into the thoughts and reasoning of all family members. This is a way to shape your teaching of such topics as friendship, honesty, community-building, interdependence, education, goal-setting, loyalty, etiquette, kindness, following the rules, spirituality, money, bravery, health, and many more issues you care to discuss.

Teaching comes into play because you are not simply using the forum to have adults ask and children answer questions, but to have adults answer and discuss their perspectives as well. Establishing family discussions in this manner will set the stage for open communications in your children's later years. Most parents want teenagers and young adults to talk to them, but much of the time they have not set the stage for dialogue during the younger years. Using dinner time, for example, in this manner not only gives your children a platform for answering questions but also furthers the cause of bonding them to the family unit.

BOOKS WITH QUESTIONS AND CONVERSATION-STARTERS

Several books can take your family from the day-to-day events of your lives to the bigger picture, with a focus that shows concern beyond the scope of your household:

For many years I have used *The Kids' Book of Questions* by Gregory Stock for questions as part of the weekly homework that I send home to families. This book was written after the author's success with *The Book of Questions*.

Bret Nicholaus and Paul Lowrie have written three books along these lines. The most useful one for families is probably *The Mom & Dad Conversation Piece: Creative Questions to Celebrate the Family*, which followed their *The Conversation Piece: Creative Questions to Tickle the Mind*. They have also written *Think Twice: An Entertaining Collection of Choices*.

Also look for *If... (Questions for the Game of Life)*, by Evelyn McFarlane and James Saywell.

SHARE YOUR THINKING

Sometimes I ask a child to tell me or the class how she figured out an answer she just gave, but she can't find the words to explain how she did it. My most successful students have been those whose parents have taken the time to talk to them — especially in the process I call sharing your thinking — verbalizing your thought process.

The idea is not to present your way as the right and only way. Explaining it as one way to come up with the answer leaves the door open for your child to come up with ways of his own.

For example, when measuring something, you might say, "It's eighteen inches long. That's a foot and a half. I know that a foot is twelve inches and that half a foot is six inches. Twelve plus six is eighteen."

Putting words with chores that you are doing adds an auditory component to the visual. This can be especially powerful if it is a job that you expect one of the children to be fulfilling soon.

As another example, it is reasonable to expect that a child in the early elementary grades can properly sort the utensils when the dishwasher is emptied. The job becomes more manageable if you have shared your thinking with the child who will be doing it:

"Now we put the silverware in this holder. We know that the soup spoons go here because this spot is shaped like the biggest spoons. I have to be careful with the forks because the space for the dinner forks is about the same size as the space for the salad forks. And the dinner forks are only a little bit bigger than the salad forks, so you have to look carefully to make sure that they don't get mixed up together."

In sharing your thinking, you are using the appropriate and necessary vocabulary, adding the auditory to the visual and kinesthetic, and giving your child the tool to be able to explain his own thinking process.

A GAME FOR THINKING — 20 QUESTIONS

You are thinking of an object and your child is trying to guess what it is. She has to guess by asking twenty questions that can be answered yes or no. A good strategy to help her with her own line of questioning is for you to model the way you can narrow down the choices. So ask *her* to think of the object for you to guess. "Is it something I can play with?" "Do we have one in our house?" "Is it in the kitchen?"

IN TOUCH WITH THE LEARNING PROCESS

A recent experience gave me an opportunity to reflect about the learning process. I took a class to learn how to use the software I purchased to design my website. I was the dunce of the class, frequently two or more steps behind my classmates. I was befuddled as the teacher gave instructions that others in the class understood, but I did not.

It reminded me of my first trip to Japan, in 1982, when I did not know a word of the language. However, during my six weeks there, I spent much time, especially on trains, looking at the writing and comparing it to phonetic translations into English. I learned to say a few phrases. By the end of the trip, I was able to say a few things in Japanese and read several signs. I was as excited as the little kid who poked his mother's arm, pointing to a billboard, and saying, "Look, mama. It's a 'e'!" (See page 15.)

These experiences have served me well. I became sensitized to the joy that children feel when they are learning, as well as the need for the teacher to make sure that all children are understanding instructions.

Adults who continue to be learners can realize two benefits. First of all, we become role models to the young people in our lives. Secondly, when we are in the position of student, it helps us to understand what it is like for children to be learning.

I once heard in a lecture that in 1899, the United States Patent Office made a statement that must have seemed to make sense at the time: everything that could possibly be invented had already been invented.

Looking back over the last 100 years, we can see the folly of such a statement. Yet, many of us approach our own lives with the attitude that we have already learned everything that we need to learn.

Whether you are a parent or a teacher, these are points to which you can be attuned. Your awareness of the learner's frame of mind can make a difference in his ability to continue learning and feel an accomplishment.

EQUAL OPPORTUNITIES FOR BOTH SEXES

Much has been written and spoken, especially since the Seventies, about the women's movement, feminism, and equality of the sexes. For me, the bottom line is that in the classroom, and especially in the public schools that are funded by taxpayer monies, all children have equal opportunities and equal access to education.

What it does not mean, however, is that we will deny that there are certain inclinations that boys and girls have when placed in social contexts. For examples, girls may prefer to play with dolls and boys may prefer to play with blocks, but it does not mean that we tell boys that they are not allowed to play with dolls and that we tell girls that they are not allowed to play with blocks.

When I was in junior high school, only boys took shop class and only girls took home economics. Since that time, many communities have recognized that the skills to be learned in these classes are useful for the members of both sexes, and that they have equal access to these courses.

Similarly, when I was growing up, it was mostly men who went into medicine and law. Women predominated, and still do, as teachers in elementary school classrooms, with about 85% of all classes at that level taught by them.

Does this mean that men should be denied the possibility of being elementary school teachers and that women should be steered away from law and medicine?

I hope that parents will support their children's interests in hobbies, studies, and other pursuits by looking beyond the age-old stereotypes that link tasks to the mainstream sex of the people who do those tasks.

WHAT WE CALL OUR KIDS

"I'm a picky eater," one of my students told me when we were sitting near each other while eating lunch during a field trip. Her parents had told her this, which, in turn, gave her permission to continue to be exactly that.

What are some of the things that you call your children when they can hear you say it? I advise you to be careful about what you call them, because they will, more often than not, find a way to live up to what you call them.

If you call your child shy, it gives him permission not to extend his hand in friendship to other children. After all, he's shy. You told him that. Now he is living up to it.

What other names are you using about your children in their presence? Troublemaker? Class clown? Tomboy? Go-getter? Lady's man? All-boy? Princess?

The power of these words has its effect not only on children but on adults as well. One day, while sitting together in our yard, I noticed something that was broken and needed to be fixed. I don't even remember what it was. But I do remember the words my spouse used and the effect of those words on me: As I got up to take care of the problem, I was called "a man of action."

Those words propelled me into future action, too. I felt that I now had a title I needed to live up to. I got things done around the house. After all, I was a man of action, and a man of action gets things done.

Sure, after a while it became a household joke. But it became part of the way that I saw myself. And if those words can have that kind of an effect to somebody who is older than fifty, imagine what their impact must be on a youngster!

WORDS HAVE AN IMPACT

You may remember a popular poem, "Children Learn What They Live," that was popular on posters in the seventies. Its author, Dorothy Law Nolte, has turned it into a valuable little book for parents. Called *Children Learn What They Live: Parenting to Inspire Values*, it is packed with down-home wisdom.

FAMILY MISSION STATEMENT

What are the values that your family holds? Taking time to think and talk about them is a way for parents to convey them to their children. This communication also engenders a sense of belonging to the group, as all the members work toward the same goals.

An effective way to work on this would be the following process:

- The parents talk between themselves about what is important to them.

- The parents tell their children about these values.

- The entire family discusses the values so that everyone understands them.

- The family's actions match the stated values.

Let's say, for example, that the parents feel that eating dinner together at least six nights a week is something that they want to do in order to foster a sense of togetherness among the members of the family and for everyone to communicate with each other during those meals.

Once the parents have decided that this is an approach they want to take, they tell their children and have a family discussion about it, possibly at the dinner table. They help the children to understand what the benefits are when all members of the family do this.

They may follow this up by having a set dinner time, by asking for children's suggestions in planning the meal, or, depending on the ages of children, by having them help in some way with meal preparation.

If they put their efforts toward making this an enjoyable time for family members to enjoy each other's company and gather family solidarity from it, then the children will continue to value the time together.

The family mission statement can cover a wide diversity of values to be decided, first by the parents and then by all members. Consider any of these topics for inclusion in yours:

- the way money will be saved and spent

- the importance of education

- the amount of family time you will spend together

- the importance of activities outside the home and school

- the responsibilities each member of the family will have toward maintaining the household

Keep in mind that the earlier these values are discussed and established within the family, the easier they will be able to follow as children grow into their teenage years.

HELP FROM AN EXPERT

Stephen R. Covey discusses the value of having a mission statement in his bestselling book, *The 7 Habits of Highly Effective People*, (1989), New York: Fireside, Simon and Shuster. This is Habit 2, Begin with the end in mind. In this principle, he says, "To begin with the end in mind means to start with a clear understanding of your destination. It means to know where you're going so that you better understand where you are now and so that the steps you take are always in the right direction." (page 98)

WHAT YOU SAY ABOUT WORK

Children hear what their parents say about their jobs. They form opinions about their own work (school) and their future job by what they hear their working parents say.

Positive talk about work encourages children to understand that the education they are receiving will have a worthwhile outcome. After all, why work hard at school if ultimately it is going to lead to a job that you hate, working with people you don't get along with, or for a boss who is a tyrant?

Share stories about your work and encourage children to tell stories about their work. Use vocabulary related to your job. This broadens the perspective about your job and increases your child's vocabulary.

A critical quality we can impart to our young people as we consider possible career paths is the curiosity to be interested in learning new things. After all, many of our young people will find themselves in jobs that do not even exist today. Therefore, it is not possible to train them for specific jobs while they are still in elementary school.

What we can do, however, is encourage them to be lifelong learners. In that way, if they are always interested in learning, they will be able to follow the lead wherever technological advances and societal needs take them.

When adults gossip about co-workers, we teach children that it is all right to gossip about their classmates. In contrast, when we explain that we went to the person with whom we had a problem, and we worked out the solution, we teach our children that this is the approach we expect them to take.

If your job involves maintaining the confidentiality of a client or patient, this is something that your children should understand and respect. Model this is an example to your children.

Finally, be sure to impart to your children the important values of arriving at work on time, completing assignments on time, and showing respect to all co-workers (in their case, classmates). Parents have a tremendous influence in these areas, and teachers are counting on you to use it.

YOU'RE GOING TO COLLEGE!

The mom of one of my students recently gave me a copy of a column by Jane Bryant Quinn, the nationally syndicated columnist who writes about financial issues. It is related to two topics that are dear to me: going to college and saving money for that crucial education.

The fact that your child is going to college should be a given, considering our society and our times. This is true regardless of your family's finances or socioeconomic status.

Whether parents have gone to college or not, family discussions about education should be imbued with the understanding that college will follow high school just as surely as first grade follows kindergarten. Parents need to infuse the conversation with the attitude that the family will make it happen.

Parents who are college graduates can speak about their own college experiences. Studying, roommates, writing term papers, all-nighters, organizations, and jobs are all valuable topics in their own way. Additionally, make it your business to visit college campuses so your children can get a sense of the diversity that exists; this can be done either in the area near your home or when you travel to other parts of the country.

The mom who gave me the column admits that her family hasn't done much to save for their child's college education. With other financial demands on them, they recently took to culling their coins regularly and have begun saving the newly-minted quarters that feature the states. They are also collecting Bicentennial quarters.

Thus, their child is included in the process and is learning about geography and history at the same time.

PLANS FOR SAVING

The article by Ms. Quinn focuses on information about Section 529 of the Internal Revenue Code, which was authorized in 1996. It empowers each state to enact its own version of a college savings plan. There are 41 participating states. You can get more information from *The Best Way to Save for College* by Joseph Hurley, 1-800-487-7624, www.savingforcollege.com or get information about your state's plan at 1-877-277-6496, www.collegesavings.org.

TEACHING GRATITUDE

Being thankful is always in season. It's not just for Thanksgiving.

In November, I assign my students a homework writing journal that includes daily entries that begin, "I am thankful for...." This is as good a time as any to help your children reflect on something for which they, too, are grateful.

Taking time to talk as a family about your gratitude can lead you to realize that you can leave your personal comfort zone to take up a cause to help other people. There are many ways that this can be accomplished. These are some that I have used successfully in my classroom:

- My students were touched by an appeal from the Junior Girl Scout troop at our school. The Scouts were collecting clothing and toys to send to people who had been devastated by Hurricane Mitch in Central America. It made a big impression on my six-year-olds that so many children had lost everything they owned. "Even their toys?" one child asked. They could identify with this.

- During the month preceding World AIDS Day on the first of December, we collect pennies to contribute to San Francisco's AIDS Emergency Fund. We have also, on occasion, taken the opportunity to count and wrap the pennies before we hand them over. At first the kids thought that a few pennies here and there didn't mean very much. But after a few weeks, the jar is so heavy that nobody in the class could pick it up. It's a visible lesson that shows the meaning of collective power.

- The Leukemia Society of America appealed to many schools to collect money for children with leukemia. Spurred on by their visual success that they had experienced only a few months before, my students enthusiastically brought in their coins for this cause.

Perhaps a discussion with your own family can lead to a program toward which you would like to lend a hand. Whatever it is, you can help your children to widen their world view by seeing that they can do something to make life more comfortable for others. More importantly, it enhances children's feelings of self-worth. Children feel good about themselves when they have helped others.

Kids are masterful at zeroing in on what they don't have and what they think they have to get. Thanksgiving is a good time to challenge that line of thinking - to help them appreciate what they have rather than mourn what they are missing. Since parents have been on the planet much longer, you have a wider perspective than then children. This is a good time to share your wisdom with your little ones.

We have a choice about how we look at our lives. I choose to focus on what I have, as opposed to what I want. I like this quotation attributed to Meister Eckhart (1260? - 1327): "When we think about what we have, we always have enough. When we think about what we want, we never have enough."

Every household chore is an opportunity to serve as a reminder of appreciation. While washing the dishes, focus on gratitude for the meal just eaten, the family members with whom we shared it, and the kitchen in which it was prepared. While making the bed, be grateful for the bed itself. Doing the laundry makes me think about having a selection of clothes to clean, as well as the family members who wear each item. Children will not necessarily see these connections; it is up to us to point them out.

SHARING THOUGHTS ABOUT GRATITUDE

There are so many different ways that we can share our thoughts on this topic with our children. Here is one of them:

As the family sits down to a meal together, start with one member and go around the table. Everyone takes a turn to mention something for which she or he is grateful. How many times can you go around the table? The children will delight in hearing that they are on your list!

Children's contributions to others, either in person or through an organized fundraising effort, can help them adjust their view so that it includes people beside themselves.

Try this magic fairy approach. Your magic wand touches one possession after another. As it does, your child has to imagine that the object disappears from her life, never to return. What would that be like? Perhaps it will inspire a renewed appreciation for what she has.

LIMIT TELEVISION AND MOVIES

Parents have supreme influence in their children's lives. Parents control the most important elements: where the family lives, what they eat, and what they do. When I talk about creating an attitude for lifelong learning, it is just a matter of time before I have to broach the subject of television.

This isn't to say that television can't be used well as a learning tool. It can. But the majority of what is on television is *not* educational by any means. Much of what children see on television includes:

• violence

• illegal acts

• illicit acts

• smart-alecky kids disrepecting adults

• shows in which the entire plot exists only because people don't tell each other the truth about what is going on

Near the end of April, TV-Free America is sponsors National TV-Turnoff Week. TV-Free America has compiled impressive statistics about the TV-watching habits of Americans. For example, the average American child, ages 2-11, watches television 1,197 minutes per week. In contrast, the average parents spend 38.5 minutes per week in meaningful conversation with their children. While 25% of teenagers can name Philadelphia as the city where the US constitution was written, 75% know that the ZIP code 90210 is Beverly Hills.

Keeping this in mind, here are some ideas for guiding your child's television viewing:

What do you do instead? Here is a partial list of some things you can do instead of watching TV: play games, read, jump rope, build things, write letters or stories, put on a play or puppet show, visit people, plant flowers or a tree, take a walk or hike, listen to music, dance or sing, tell stories, practice musical instruments, keep a journal, create art, clean out your closet, visit your public library, bake something, rearrange your furniture, have a garage sale, fix something, put photos into a family album.

- Allow a maximum amount of time each day. For example, children under five years old get half an hour. Children up to eight get one hour. Or come up with a formula that suits your family. I have had students whose parents do not allow television watching on weekdays and a maximum of two hours during the weekend.

- Make sure that all chores and homework are completed before watching television.

- Monitor what your children watch on television.

- In the event that a time-out or other disciplinary measure does not work, take away television viewing time.

- Keep the television(s) turned off when you are not watching.

- Be a role model: keep your own time in front of the television set limited.

- Never let the television take the place of books, educational games, family time, exercising, or creative activities.

MOVING AWAY FROM THE TV

There are many resources available if you would like to turn elsewhere for your family activities:

- TV-Free America (202-887-0436, www.tvfa.org). Their Organizer's Kit includes information for organizing a TV-turnoff, lists of family activities, impressive statistics about family life, children and education, violence and health, commercialism, general information about the impact of television on our lives, and reprints of several articles about TV-turnoff from newspapers and magazines.

- Adams Media Corp. (800-872-5627, www.adamsonline.com), publishers of *365 TV-Free Activities You Can Do with Your Child* by Steve & Ruth Bennett, an outstanding resource of ideas that capitalize on the use of time and common household objects to focus on family members spending time together. The goal is to relate to each other, rather than looking at the television.

- *Four Arguments for the Elimination of Television*, by Jerry Mander is a scholarly work that carefully analyzes the effects of television on its viewers.

- *Family Fun Book*, by Joni Hilton has no anti-television agenda, but its sub-title gives you a hint as to what it is about: *More than 400 Amazing, Amusing, and All-Around Awesome Activities for the Entire Family.*

INCLUDING CHILDREN IN SOLVING FAMILY PROBLEMS

What group of people living in the same household doesn't have problems? When adults take the lead in solving problems in a calm and methodic way, they are giving their children a useful tool that they take with them wherever they go. And believe me, whichever approach you take does carry over into the classroom!

I offer this sequence to help you find solutions with your family members:

1. Figure out what the problem is. Each person has a different perspective, so listen carefully to what everyone has to say. Encourage a safe atmosphere where each person's opinion is accepted and valued.

2. Talk about what you are currently doing about the problem. Maybe you are not doing anything — just letting it continue as it is. You may be surprised at some family members' responses to what you are doing!

3. Brainstorm all the possible solutions to the problem. Accept all answers. It doesn't mean that you will necessarily use them all. Your little ones may have way-out suggestions. Write down all of them.

4. Decide as a group to get behind one of the solutions. Everyone has to agree to be part of the same approach and give it a chance to work. This may be difficult if one or more person is emotionally attached to his solution.

5. Give it a try for at least a week. This will give you a chance to see if it is working. Get everyone's agreement — especially those who were lobbying for other solutions.

6. Plan a meeting at the end of the week to evaluate how the solution is working. At this time you can decide to continue with the same actions or switch to other ones.

Having everyone work together on solutions to problems helps to create a feeling of solidarity in the family. After all, you are all on the same team! Not only that, but in this process, two messages that you convey to your children will serve them well for many years to come:

1. The key to your success is in your own hands. When you take responsibility for your actions, you make your success happen. Nobody else can do this for you.

2. If you have a plan, you cannot fail. You decide what your plan is and figure out step by step how to make it work.

CHAPTER 9:
RESPONSIBILITY

SETTING LIMITS

I sent for an audiocassette of a speech given by Dr. Sylvia Rimm, a nationally syndicated child psychologist. She has sage advice about setting limits for children, and I offer you the classroom perspective on the subject.

The classroom is a place where a child who has not learned limits can play out an almost-daily drama that has a negative impact on the entire class. This is the child who has to have the pink scissors, not the blue ones. She has to get her choice of partners from among the other classmates. She is the child for whom the whole world is Burger King: the place where she can have it her way.

And while she is making a fuss, what is happening to the other children in the classroom? The educational process is shut down for everyone. The remainder of the class becomes bystanders to the power struggle that ensues. The teacher must be careful not to give this struggling child everything she asks for lest any of the other children try the same tactic, reasoning, "But you let her have it when she cried for it."

Dr. Rimm advises that parents need to offer their children leadership, limits, and love. By having limits imposed on them by their parents, children learn that they cannot get everything that they want.

By being leaders, parents have to realize that they are the ones with the wisdom. Parents have the "big picture." Parents — and teachers as well — have to understand that when kids say, "I hate you" because they are not getting what they want, that this is an immediate and temporary feeling that later subsides. Children crave limits. In being on the receiving end, they understand that parents are really showing their love this way.

Most importantly, Dr. Rimm advises, children receive small amounts of responsibility and choices when they are younger. These increase as the children grow older and can take on more. To give too much choice and responsibility at too early an age is detrimental to children.

Leave everything a little better than you found it.

— H. Jackson Brown, Jr.

HELP FROM AN EXPERT

Dr. Sylvia Rimm, a child psychologist, is a frequent guest on the Today Show and a syndicated columnist. She has written more than a dozen books. I can highly recommend *Dr. Sylvia Rimm's Smart Parenting: How to Parent So Children Will Learn* and *Sylvia Rimm on Raising Kids.*

TEACHING RESPONSIBILITY

"Can you drive me to school today?" Elizabeth asked. She wasn't running late. There was plenty of time to walk or take her bike. I could have driven her to school, but I resisted. This was something she needed to do for herself.

I think about children taking responsibilities at home in much the same way as I think of using muscles to exercise. With the muscles, if we use them regularly, they get stronger. If we don't, they atrophy.

Likewise with responsibilities: if children have small jobs when they are younger, and these jobs grow with them, they become stronger people. Their sense of self is well-developed and they grow up with a can-do attitude.

Here are three examples of ways we can help build this important quality into our children's character.

- You wonder what homework papers your child has brought home. Resist the urge to let your fingers do the walking through her backpack. This is an area where it would be best to have your child be in charge. Sit with her as she takes everything out, shows you what assignments need to be done, asks you to sign any papers that need to go back to school, and then puts everything back together for the following day.

- Your children are constantly asking about upcoming events, unclear as to how much time will pass until they come. Don't take on this burden yourself. A family calendar, posted on the refrigerator or other place accessible to children, can do this for you. Each member of the family puts her or his activities on the calendar with a marker of a color that designates whose it is. This way, children can track their own activities and learn how to read a calendar.

- The kids are hungry. Is it reasonable to have you wait on them every time? Why not designate certain foods as the ones that are most acceptable for between-meal snacks, put them in an accessible place, and let them serve themselves? Make sure you have a clear understanding of the way you expect the area to be cleaned after they have finished.

GIVING AND KEEPING YOUR WORD

Children are learning how to deal with a wide variety of people in their lives: siblings, cousins, classmates, parents, grandparents, neighbors, teachers. In working out the dynamics of all these relationships, there are bound to be problems such as hitting, talking back, and taking things that don't belong to them.

Many books have been written about the pros and cons of punishing, spanking, and getting kids to do what they should do. In my experience, stating the rules and getting children to agree that they will follow them has been an effective way of getting cooperation from little ones. When a mistake has been make, I have had good results in having children make a commitment toward positive behavior in the future.

When there is a problem, I have found that children generally respond well to having a heartfelt talk with the adult in charge, be it the parent or the teacher. Most children want to do what is right. An explanation of what is right comes from the adult.

Of course, the words will be different if you are talking to a four-year-old than if you are talking to an eight-year-old, but the tenor of the talk is the same: you are a member of a group, whether it is a class at school or a family at home, and all the members of the group need to contribute certain behaviors if things are to function well. Then you ask if the child understands what you are talking about and agrees that the behavior will change in the future. Most children understand this dynamic.

I have found that writing down the commitment can be a powerful tool in helping the child to achieve it. At home, we have *The Book of Understandings*. This eliminates the child's telling us, "We never talked about that," or "I don't remember talking about that."

An example from our own book is that on March 7, 1995, Brian signed a statement that he understood that he did not have permission to change the outgoing message in the answering machine. Since that time, he has kept his word.

Kids especially understand this when parents give some examples of the times that they make an agreement and keep their word. After all, as your children's role model in this arena, haven't you kept your agreement to do many things? Think of all those parties, athletic events, and shopping trips you said you would do... and did. Your contributions to the family have helped to keep things running smoothly. You are doing nothing more than asking your young people to follow your lead and do the same.

TAKING RESPONSIBILITY FOR YOUR MISTAKES

Many children do not own up to their mistakes for fear of being punished. Their fear is justified if parents have approached them with punishing consequences instead of viewing mistakes as learning experiences.

In my classroom, there is one statement that my students hear me say every time I am helping them get to the bottom of sticky situations: I respect people who tell me the truth. I sometimes see puzzled looks from children who have not heard an adult say something like this to them before.

Young people want to please the adults in their life. They want to see that their actions earn respect from adults.

With many children, punishment simply begets anger, resentment, and a resolve to get even with the punishing adult. If you can approach your children's mistakes with an attitude of education rather than of punishment, it will help them to be more forthright about their errors.

These are three possible outcomes that children may choose when they have made a mistake:

- lie, deny, or cover up; they usually do this for fear of reprisal. Overly harsh punishments will frequently get this type of response from children. But if you establish with your youngster that you value the truth, you will usually get it.

- parrot an apology; they tell you what you want to hear. I refer to it as parroting an apology because the words are what the adult wants, but there is no sincere meaning behind them.

- admit what they did and apologize sincerely; this is the most direct path toward building character and changing future actions.

To encourage children to come clean when they err, there are several lessons that parents can explain:

- Each of us — adults included — makes mistakes.

- We grow into being better people after we admit our mistakes and apologize sincerely to the offended party.

- A person who makes mistakes is still worthy of love and respect.

- We can forgive ourselves the same way that we forgive others.

- Nobody can be perfect. It is more important to have an attitude about learning from mistakes than not to make them in the first place.

- We live in a society based on interdependence; we count on each other for respect and the truth.

Not only do we have to live with other people: we have to be able to live with ourselves and the consequences of our actions.

JOBS AROUND THE HOUSE

Parents need to make sure that children make contributions toward the family and its home. At every age, there are things that children can do to contribute to the household community. Some examples follow:

Toddlers

Toddlers can put things away when they have finished using them. The things that they use - their clothes, toys, and books - can be put into baskets, drawers, or on the shelves that you provide for them. The key is that parents provide a place that is accessible to them.

Ages 3 - 5

Children ages 3 - 5 can dress themselves, keep their room in an orderly manner, and work with an adult or older sibling in making their bed. When you are out and about with them, see to it that they are responsible for transporting their own belongings. They can help around the house, usually under the watchful eye of the parent who is training them to contribute.

Ages 6 - 8

These children are already on the right path if they have been helping through the previous stages with you. But if they have not, it does not mean that they can't begin learning. Children of this age crave routine and structure.

They should be responsible for all grooming such as bathing, brushing their teeth, and washing their face and hands regularly; the only exception would be a complicated hair style that an adult has agreed to prepare.

Papers from school and all homework should be put in a routine place so that there is no question as to where to find it. Likewise, all the things that go to and from school - backpack, lunch box, sweater, umbrella, school library books - have a place assigned to them.

I like the approach that the parents of one of my students told me they followed for gifts that their children received: no toy was played with, no book read, and no new clothing worn until the child wrote a thank-you note to the person who gave it.

Ages 9 - 11

There is an assortment of things that children these ages can do fairly independently. With regard to school, they should be responsible for being sure that all homework is completed in a timely fashion. If they have a long-range assignment with multiple things that have to be done for completion, it would be most helpful if parents helped them to create a timeline of things that needed to be done and the goals for completion of these tasks. This sets a good example and helps to avoid last-minute late-night sessions before the due date.

Direct contributions toward the family can include sweeping or vacuuming shared areas, washing dishes or emptying the dishwasher, and laundering their own clothing and bed linens.

Jobs to consider for your children to do around the house:

- dusting with a cloth or feather duster

- setting or clearing the table

- sorting laundry before and/or after it is washed

- delivering laundry to the proper rooms

- vacuuming

- helping the cook — measuring, cleaning up spills

- cleaning up after meals: carrying dishes, loading dishwasher, collecting silverware, sorting silverware from dishwasher

- caring for the family pet(s) — feeding, changing water, cleaning cages, walking

Children who contribute at home feel like valued members of the household. They don't have a sense of entitlement that comes when everyone else is doing things for them. They take this attitude with them to the classroom, where they strive to be a productive member of that community as well.

IDEAS FOR EVERY AGE

For a complete approach to helping children with being organized and responsible in the family setting, I recommend *Ages and Stages of Getting Children Organized*, a booklet by Marcia Ramsland. It is available by sending $5.00 and a double-stamped envelope to Life Management Skills, 13726 Camino Del Suelo, San Diego, CA 92129-4430, www.OrganizingPro.com

ORGANIZED FOR SUCCESS

Helping kids to be organized when they are young can lead to their being more productive when they are older. Many children have too many possessions crammed into their closets, drawers, and all over their rooms. Time spent working with the family to weed out unwanted and unneeded excess in their rooms is productive. Your children probably have more books, clothing, and toys than they need or want, so help them to sort through it all.

One way to appeal to children to weed out such articles is to explain that there are other people who need and can use what they don't: children who have no books of their own, very few toys, or a limited selection of clothing from which to choose.

There are three major benefits of this activity. First of all, your child has a sense of contributing to another person. Secondly, this frees up some space for navigating more freely in his own room. Thirdly, you teach the lesson that it is all right to get rid of things.

All three of these benefits can become habits in later life and be sources of joy as children grow up and establish households of their own. Contrast this to the mentality many of us have concerning the collection and retention of material possessions: many of us who either lived through or are children of people who lived through the Great Depression, have been schooled in the opposite philosophy, as we stockpile possessions that are no longer useful or necessary.

If your community has a wide-scale effort, such as a city-wide garage sale, get involved at the same time as everyone else is doing the same activity. Whatever you do, though, make sure that your kid doesn't spend the day checking out other garage sales and loading up on more junk!

HELP IN GETTING ORGANIZED

Do you need help getting organized? You're not alone. More than one thousand members of the National Association of Professional Organizers (NAPO) are here to help. Founded in 1985, this group has chapters and individual members all over the United States and in several other countries. If you need a referral to professional organizer near you, NAPO can be reached at P. O. Box 140647, Austin, TX 78714-0647, telephone 512-454-8626, www.napo.net.

CLOTHING SENDS A MESSAGE

100% MISCHIEF: this is the caution printed across a sweatshirt worn by a kindergartner at the school where I teach. I guess his parents are trying to tell us something. My fantasy is that when his teacher calls home to talk about a problem, the parents tell her, "We warned you about him." Then they're off the hook!

Similar messages that puzzle me, which I have seen on children's clothing are: HERE COMES TROUBLE , BAD TO THE BONE, and RUDE, CRUDE, AND SOCIALLY UNACCEPTABLE.

There is also one that has no words with it, but is stunning just the same: little girls dressed like streetwalkers.

What are parents saying when they dress their children this way?

Children are sponges. They absorb into their psyches the values that their parents demonstrate to them through words, deeds, and attitudes.

Above all, children hear what we say about them. Most of the time, they will live up (or down, as the case may be) to our expectations of them. Why give them low expectations?

When they are given permission to misbehave, they begin to believe (1) that they have no control over their behavior, and (2) that the only attention they can get is the negative behavior that parents have told the world to expect of them.

Do we really want to tell our boys that we expect them to misbehave, thereby giving them permission to go ahead and get it out of their systems? If the "boys will be boys" attitude starts when they are younger, what will be condoned as they get older? Drunk driving? Sexual harassment? Fun and games with guns and knives?

And if we dress our girls as harlots with makeup, tight clothing, and showing lots of bare skin — all before they reach puberty — what types of sophistication will they need to seek when they reach adolescence? Smoking? Drinking? Pregnancy?

I suggest that parents be mindful of the media images to which they expose their children. They also need to exercise their parental controls, which includes considering the messages that parents themselves are sending about their youngsters' appearance and behavior.

CHAPTER 10:
COOPERATION WITH OTHERS

TEACHING ABOUT CARING

On the fourth day of school, one of my first-graders was rocking in his chair and fell out of it. Several of his classmates laughed. There was one dissenting voice, however: a girl, not yet six years old, objected, "It's not nice to laugh. He might be hurt."

There were three things I wanted to do immediately: (1) make sure that the boy was not hurt (he wasn't); (2) show appreciation for the compassion of his one classmate; (3) conduct a class discussion about concern for the feelings of others in situations such as this.

Children watch a lot of television and movies. In both live action and cartoons, there is a tremendous amount of screen time given to people falling, dropping things, getting wet, and other forms of physical comedy created for the amusement of the audience.

Young children have not had enough experience to distinguish among these differing situations. It seems perfectly natural, therefore, for six-year-olds to assume that since it is all right to laugh at the people they see on the screen, that it is all right to laugh at people who do the same things right in front of them.

At that moment, I thought about a song that was fairly new to me at that time. I had recently discovered a book entitled *Love Can Build a Bridge*, by Naomi Judd. It included a cassette with The Judds singing the song by the same name. I was attracted to the text as well as the winsome illustrations: children of many cultures shown helping each other.

I played the cassette and showed the pictures. The lyrics include these: "Love can build a bridge between your heart and mine. Love can build a bridge. Don't you think it's time? Don't you think it's time?"

Almost every day since then, somebody in the class asks me to play it so the class can sing along. I think it will be a way for me to help get across the message of caring for others during the current school year.

Treat others the way you would want them to treat you.

— The Golden Rule

We have committed the Golden Rule to memory; let us now commit it to life.

— Edwin Markham

125

GOOD MANNERS

In 1999, the Louisiana Senate voted 34-5 that elementary school students are to answer their teachers with either, "Yes, sir" or "Yes, ma'am," "No, sir" or "No, ma'am." This came at the behest of Governor Mike Foster.

The ability to get along with others is a skill that everyone needs to learn in order to be successful in our society. Parents can greatly enhance this ability by teaching their children basic manners.

One of the first things about which I talk to my students early in the school year is the use of the phrase "May I please..." at the beginning of any request they have. After a few weeks of trying this, I then no longer respond if a child does not include it. Instead, I sit there with a blank stare, waiting, until I hear that phrase first.

The phrase I teach for those children asking others to do something for them is "Would you please..." A phrase such as this sets up the listener for cooperation rather than antagonism.

You'd be surprised how few children have been taught to express their thanks when receiving something! When I hand out snacks in the beginning of the school year, there may be as few as 3 children in a class of twenty who say this without being coached. By the end of the year, it's 100%.

Not surprisingly, the children who begin the school year with basic manners have lots more going for them as well: parents who attend parent-teacher conferences, parents who help make sure homework is handed in, parents who read to them at home.

These are the children who don't get into fights, who show acts of kindness to others, who consider the feelings of their classmates, who navigate through the world in placid waters. This can be done without legislation!

Parents are, of course, the adults with whom children have the greatest opportunities to see interacting politely with other people. If parents act an in uncivilized way, they are setting a bad example for their children to follow. Not only that: they are setting up themselves to be on the receiving end of their own children's backtalk, bad manners, and rude behavior.

If things have gotten out of hand, it may be time to have a family meeting to discuss not only the children's behavior, but your own as well. Confessing to your own children that your behavior may not have been exemplary is setting a good example to them in two ways: (1) It gives them permission to admit when they are wrong. (2) It shows that polite behavior is something that needs to be in effect not only when they are children, but when they will be adults, so this is a lifelong skill they are learning.

RESOLVING CONFLICTS

When interpersonal conflicts arise among students, children need peaceful solutions. I know that some parents encourage children to defend themselves physically. But teachers can't be in position to referee fistfights. For that reason, many teachers encourage children to solve their problems by using their words. In this way, we keep our hands, feet, and objects to ourselves.

Parents have told me that when children learn to use problem-solving techniques successfully at school, it frequently carries over to use with siblings. The goal is for children to be able to solve their disputes without adult intervention. In any event, parents, teachers, classmates, and siblings benefit when children are empowered in this way.

• The first step in the process is the statement of displeasure: "I don't like it when you take my pencil."

• Then comes the statement for the desired outcome: "I want you to give it back to me."

• It is sometimes helpful to ask, "Why are you doing this?" or "What do you want?"

I sometimes see that when a child comes to me with a problem ("Joey scratched me."), the complainer tells me he has no idea why it happened. When I work with the children, I often find out that Joey scratched Mikey because Mikey took Joey's toy. Mikey conveniently forgot what he had done to instigate Joey.

I do not spend a lot of time asking children to apologize to each other after an altercation. In my experience, children are usually not sorry about what they did. If they are not sorry, what would be the point in making them say that they are? I don't want to make the situation worse by asking them to lie.

Instead of a focus on the incident that has already happened, I prefer a commitment toward future positive behavior, such as a promise not to hit again or to solve the next situation with words. I explain that I expect them to keep their word to me, just as I keep my word when I make promises to them. In this way, we bring an honorable closure to a tough situation.

COMMUNITY SERVICE

"The greatest good you can do for another is not just share your riches, but to reveal to him his own." Benjamin Disraeli

One of the cornerstones of a healthy community is involvement on the part of its residents. When we make an effort to get to know others better, we have an expanded and more complex view of our community.

Young people involved in community service are less likely to be engaged in the destructive behaviors of using drugs, joining gangs, and getting pregnant. Their school dropout rate is lower and they are motivated to achieve higher grades in high school.

Community service also helps children and teens to learn about an abundance of social issues such as understanding of the environment and interaction with diverse groups of people. Most important, in my opinion, is the awareness of their own interdependence with other people in the society.

Some programs through which young people and their families can contribute their time include homes for the disabled and aging, libraries, hospitals, homeless shelters, and schools.

But it is not necessary to join a structured program in order to participate in a form of community service. Individuals can do any number of things to connect with others toward the end of touching and improving their lives: send a note or card of encouragement to a friend or family member, call a lonely person, do a household chore or shopping for somebody who needs assistance, or brighten another person's day with flowers. Individual tutoring of a younger neighborhood child who needs help with reading, writing or math is a fine way to enhance the self esteem of the people on both sides of the equation.

Albert Einstein said, "Only a life lived for others is a life worthwhile." This leads to one of the greatest benefits of community service, especially for teenagers: it gets them to take the focus off themselves and onto others. Time and thought spent away from shopping, clothing, appearance, television, movies, and dating can be channeled into the needs and circumstances of other people.

CHAPTER 11:
PHYSICAL WELLBEING

LET'S GET PHYSICAL

Don't let the temperature and number of hours of light affect your outdoor activities. An article in the *San Jose Mercury News* in the fall of 1998 reported that ten million children in the U.S. are overweight — a record high.

There are many things you can do to help ensure that your child keeps in shape. A sound body contributes greatly to your child's mental health and readiness to learn in school.

- Make short trips in town a family affair - and leave the car at home! There are many places to which you can walk, take bikes, or use inline skates: friends' homes, neighborhood shopping, nearby parks, school.

- Expand your family's activities to include new ventures. If you haven't hiked together near your home, add this to your repertoire. If there is paddleboating at a local lake, try that: it gets those feet moving!

- Set a cooperative tone in your approach to exercise. With a variety of ages of children and different abilities of the adults, nobody has to win. You're all having fun together as you keep in shape. For fun non-competitive games, look for *The New Games Book* by the New Games Foundation.

- Many parents have discovered the ease of having children's parties outside the house — less mess to clean up at home. As long as you are out, have the kids set up and put themselves through an obstacle course. (And have them help take it down, too.)

- Make sure your child is wearing clothing that is appropriate for physical activity. Most girls are more comfortable in pants or shorts, rather than dresses, for this. And pay special attention to footwear. Sturdy athletic shoes give the support and stability that are not offered by sandals, jellies, boots, or dressy shoes with no traction.

Even though children may have a supervised physical education class at school, remember that they have a morning recess and lunch recess every day, so they should be dressed for comfort during their daily physical activity.

A healthy body is a guest-chamber for the soul; a sick body is a prison.

— Francis Bacon

THE IMPORTANCE OF BREAKFAST

We have all heard that breakfast is the most important meal of the day. Adelle Davis, author of *Let's Eat Right to Keep Fit*, extolled the virtues that I remember ever since I read her book in the Seventies: "Eat breakfast like a king, lunch like a prince, and dinner like a pauper."

We teachers see the result of children's breakfast eating habits - especially when they do not have a decent breakfast at home: headaches, tummyaches, and lack of ability to concentrate are chief among them.

What if your child doesn't take to the traditional breakfast fare? We have hit upon an unusual solution at our house: Elizabeth's favorite breakfast is plain pasta (any shape, no sauce) in a little margarine with parmesan cheese on top. We always have leftover pasta in containers in the refrigerator, so it is a simple matter to take out a little bit, warm it up, and offer her a complex carbohydrate that she will not only eat, but will keep her going until lunch.

If your child resists the typical assortment of cereals, toast, bagels, bread, waffles, and pancakes, perhaps you can explore this area together and come up with a solution that is easy for you to prepare that will also be something to get into that empty stomach to keep her nourished during the morning hours.

Sugar is known for providing a quick burst of energy to most people. This is a phenomenon that does not last for a long time. The simple carbohydrates in sugar are easily expended, resulting in a fairly short-lived burst. Then the body gets tired and is focused only on wanting to get something else to eat. This creates chaos when the child is supposed to be paying attention to what his teacher is saying or contributing to a group or partner activity.

Your child probably has some sort of a recess break every morning. You can reinforce the need for that important morning food by providing a snack that can be easily transported to school and eaten during this time.

HYGIENE AND CLEANLINESS

Most parents do an exemplary job in keeping their children clean and well-groomed. A healthy child is in a better frame of mind to learn than a sick child.

There are some basics that parents need to teach at home:

- Wash hands before meals and after using the bathroom. The hands are a major distributor of bacteria from one person to another.

- Cover the mouth when sneezing or coughing. We used to encourage children to cover the mouth or nose with a hand to prevent the spread of germs. Now we teach that if a tissue or handkerchief is not available that they should sneeze or cough into the v-shaped area created when the elbow is bent.

- Brush teeth two times a day and floss at least once. Healthy teeth and gums make eating a more pleasurable experience, which leads to good health.

- When sent to school, children should be able to keep neat and clean during the school day, so that they don't go home looking like a disheveled mess. This is a beginning exercise in independence when away from home.

- Bathe regularly. Many friendships are lost in school because of the smell of unkempt children. Nobody will want to play with or sit next to a child who smells bad.

- Keep foreign objects out of the mouth. There is no end to the number of germs that can be transmitted this way.

- Don't exchange brushes, combs, hats, or other objects used in hair. In some schools, hair lice spread quickly, which causes great disruption in many households as family are forced to wash clothing and bed linens.

- Don't eat things that have fallen to the floor. Some children are so hungry that they will eat about anything, even if it has hit the floor or ground.

- By all means, keep your children home when they are ill! After all, they may not be ill if other parents had done this. Sure, it causes a problem of who will care for the sick child. But keeping him home under these conditions is not only better for him, but respectful to other families. You would want them to do that for you!

THE EFFECTS OF DIET

Many children suffer at home and at school with hyperactivity, inability to focus, and a wide number of diagnoses lumped together as learning disabilities; these may include auditory processing problems and dyslexia.

Parents, often at a loss of what to do about their children's difficulties, may be ignoring the one thing that can make the most significant changes in their children's behavior: diet.

Many of the foods introduced into our diet are full of fat, salt, and sugars. They are processed and full of chemicals. At my school, the teachers escort our students to the cafeteria. I'm pleased I don't have to stay there for a long time. It's not because of the noise factor (although I do appreciate getting away from the youthful exuberance for a while). It's because I can't stand to see what the kids are eating for lunch!

Most importantly, enough research has been done to indicate clearly that in many cases, symptoms of hyperactivity, attention deficit disorder (ADD), attention deficit hyperactive disorder (ADHD), autism, asthma, and sleep disorders related to ADHD disappear altogether with the change of diet — and no additional drugs are needed.

Typical programs, like Dr. Feingold's, suggest eliminating ingredients such as artificial food dye and flavors; BHA, BHT, and TBHQ (petroleum-based preservatives); salycylates; and corn syrup.

 RESEARCH ABOUT THE LINK BETWEEN DIET AND BEHAVIOR

One of the earliest researchers in this field was Dr. Benjamin Feingold, who wrote *Why Your Child is Hyperactive.* The Feingold Association of the United States (FAUS) continues studying these issues. You can contact FAUS at 127 E. Main St. #106, Riverhead, NY 11901, phone 800-321-3287, www.feingold.org.

Other valuable books on the topic are:

Why Can't My Child Behave? Why Can't She Cope? Why Can't He Learn?, by Jane Hersey

No More Ritalin: Treating ADHD Without Drugs, by Dr. Mary Ann Block

The Myth of the A.D.D. Child: 50 Ways to Improve Your Child's Behavior and Attention Span Without Drugs, Labels, or Coercion by Thomas Armstrong.

CHAPTER 12:
PARENT INVOLVEMENT IN EDUCATION

THE SCHOOL-HOME CONNECTION

Each new school year brings me a fresh batch of twenty eager, smiling, and wiggly first-graders: your kids! This is the happy new year that I celebrate.

My first priority is to get to know these children. I establish a positive relationship with them and their families.

Schools vary in their need and desire for parental involvement. Most schools welcome it in one form or another.

Contact your child's teacher. If you have more than one school-age child, chances are you will be most needed in the class of your youngest. The younger the children in the class, the more they will need adult supervision in a variety of activities: reading groups, story time, math centers, art projects, computer tutoring, class parties, and field trips are some of the activities that need more adults than are employed in the typical classroom.

This doesn't mean you should overlook your older children. Pre-teens and teenagers will not want to be seen in your presence and will tell you that your efforts on their behalf embarrass them. At the same time, they appreciate that you care enough to spend time at their school's activities.

If you have the time, consider volunteering for school-wide activities. The PTA and site council groups have scrip sales, meetings, and a vast assortment of fund-raising opportunities awaiting the parent who would like to make a difference on the school level.

When you participate at your child's school, you are sending a vital message to her: school is important. If it is important to you, it will be important to her.

Strengthen that connection throughout the school year by attending parent-teacher conferences, open houses, science fairs, literacy fairs, school plays, and fund-raising events. Buy scrip from the PTA.

James Baldwin observed that children will not listen to their parents, but will imitate them. Take action: do something to help at your child's school.

Think of your child's education as an investment. What you put into it now will pay off in many years, and with huge dividends.

— Jay Davidson

133

RESPONSIBILITIES SCHOOLS HAVE TOWARD FAMILIES

Public education is most effective when families and schools forge a partnership and are synchronous in the process of teaching children. Each partner has responsibilities specific to its role in the child's life.

These are some responsibilities that schools have toward families. Look for these when you are searching for a school to which to send your child. The teachers and administrators should:

- Treat all members of every family with the dignity and respect that they deserve. Each of us has feelings and is trying to do our best. They should be especially welcoming in the event that younger siblings have come along to the event.

- Treat family members as equal partners in the education of the children involved. If parents need help, the school should be prepared to give it to them.

- Keep families informed about school personnel, meetings, activities, rules and expectations, classroom activities, and curriculum innovations.

- Speak in a simple manner about curriculum and expectations without the use of jargon. They should be clear. Parents are not professional educators. Many times, the curriculum is different than it was when they attended school. Teachers and administrators should be prepared to explain it in a way so that parents are comfortable in getting the skills they will need to be successful.

RESPONSIBILITIES FAMILIES HAVE TOWARD SCHOOLS

Relationships work best when each person contributes equally. It is reasonable for you to have some expectations from school officials. At the same time, there are responsibilities that families have in order to support the school. Family members should:

- Be vocal supporters of the school, its rules, and the classes that are offered. In so doing, you further the purposes of the school. If, for example, there is a rule that children should not fight in school, it would be at cross-purposes to advise your child to hit back at somebody who hits him.

- Extol the virtues of education. Talk positively about your own education and how it has helped you to be where you are today. Explain this importance to your children as well. If you are involved in continuing education classes or self-improvement of any kind, talk to this about your children in terms of how you are improving yourself, and how this will always continue.

- Talk about what happens at school every day - what your child did, learned, and talked about. When you talk about the work that you have done for the day, whether it be inside or outside of your home, explain to your child that going to school is your child's work.

- Read to your child every day. This is a ritual that begins when your child is a baby and continues through elementary school. As your child grows, have him demonstrate his reading ability by reading to you.

- Make homework part of your family routine. It must be treated as a priority in your family's life. Take into account your child's needs and learning styles. Some children work best in total silence and need to be sitting at a desk away from family activities, whereas some need background music and need to have all their supplies around them on the floor.

We must understand that the education of each child is a three-way effort that takes participation of the child, the home, and the school. The job will be done at its best when all three are working together.

GOALS FOR THE NEW SCHOOL YEAR

The week before school starts is the optimal time for the family to work together to set goals for the coming school year. Making such public statements are powerful tools that help people to bring them to fruition.

When setting goals, each member of the family takes stock in her or his actions during the last school year and looks forward to making positive changes.

Since the adults have a better understanding of this process, they go first so they can model to the children how it works.

Maybe you didn't attend any evening functions last year. One of your goals could be to go to three school events this year.

A guideline to keep in mind is to make the statement with positive words rather than negative ones. Say what you will do rather than what you won't. Instead of saying, "I won't be late to school," you say, "I will be on time to school."

Keep the goals age-appropriate. Children need to have some sense of control over what they can do.

Younger children can strive to be ready to leave the house on time every day, be responsible to hand in completed homework, remember to give papers from the teacher to parents, bring home lunchboxes and backpacks, and return library books on time.

Children in intermediate grades and middle school can pledge to pace themselves in the completion of long-term assignments, complete assignments on time, and focus more attention on subjects where grades were low last year.

High schoolers with more hectic schedules can pay attention to balancing their time among studies, jobs, dating, and extracurricular activities.

Gently talk with the kids about last year's problems and see where they can come up with suggestions for improvements. And, most of all, be there to support them in the changes for which they say they want to work.

Post them in public for all to see. The refrigerator or a bulletin board is a good place to have a regular reminder of the goals for which all of you are working.

ASSESS YOUR CHILD'S PROGRESS

When there are just a few weeks to go of the school year, many teachers begin to send home the work that has accumulated.

This is a fine time to sit down with your child and look together through the work she has done during the year. No doubt, the amount of work will be staggering: homework assignments, math papers, book reports, research projects, drawings, paintings, and other *objects d'art*.

Ask your child to talk about the work she has done. Perhaps you will find, if she is in an early grade such as kindergarten or first grade, that her writing has greatly improved during the last school year. This will be particularly evident if you have recent papers nearby to which you can compare writing from the beginning of the school year.

Slightly older children may have discovered that skills such as multiplication, which were once very difficult, have finally gotten easier, thanks to all the work that has gone into the studying.

Middle- and high-schoolers may have an increased ability in a foreign language or musical instrument. They may finally have come to an understanding of scientific concepts that had previously eluded them.

You and your child will probably not want to keep every paper that has been sent home. Use the portfolio approach common to artists: keep the pieces that show what your child considers to be her best work. These can encompass all curriculum areas — not just art.

It can be helpful for your child to verbalize reasons for keeping the objects you will be saving together. Perhaps he put a lot of work into it; he worked with a friend on it; he likes the way it came out; it got a positive comment from the teacher.

Throughout this process, your child will most appreciate that you are spending time with her in the evaluation. In doing so, you are demonstrating with your time that school is important, her efforts are important, and your time together is valuable to you.

CELEBRATING ACCOMPLISHMENTS

The completion of the school year is a good time to look at and celebrate what your child has accomplished. Also celebrate what you, as parents, accomplished, either in your child's education or furthering your own.

Children are used to having their birthday celebrated. As part of our culture, we customarily have a child blow out as many candles as he has lived years. What about using this familiar scene to extend toward the entire family's accomplishments at the completion of the school year?

Let each child determine her or his accomplishments with one candle per child: Katrina's candle symbolizes that she learned how to read, add, and subtract; she made five new friends. Josh learned his times tables, the capitals of all the states, how to shoot a basketball, and brought his homework to school on time every week.

Parents can also celebrate their contributions toward the kids' success in school. Dad went to every School Site Council meeting. Mom worked hard distributing and keeping the books for the scrip program to raise money for the school. They attended the silent auction, authors' night, the science fair, and all the parent conferences. They get candles, too!

Be sure to include any adult education that the parents completed. This is a clear message to the children that education is a life-long pursuit.

If you have the time to make the cake at home, have the children help with this project. Getting their involvement will not only heighten interest in the event, but help them with their measuring skills.

At celebration time, everyone gets a candle, takes a turn to talk about the previous school year and its accomplishments, and, after all the members of the family have had a turn to speak, everyone blows out the candles together.

It's a fine time to have everyone listen to each other and not only celebrate her own learning, but that of everyone else in the family as well.

PREPARING FOR SUMMER

As the school year approaches its close, parents, teachers and children alike have their minds on the summer. You can bet that not each of these parties has exactly the same thoughts! But summer is a good time to consider this one: how will your child maintain his academic skills so that he will be prepared for the following school year?

Your first stop is a brief meeting with his teacher. The teacher will be able to inform you if he has mastered all the skills necessary for his grade level and what needs to be done to be ready for the next one.

This is a very busy time of year for teachers. By all means, make an appointment for this meeting. You can expect that the teacher will be able to help you out in this regard, but he also needs time to be prepared to help you and your child in the best way.

If the teacher can explain the skills that need to be maintained, take that information to your nearest educational supplies store and ask the clerks there to help you find materials to use for working on these skills.

In addition to academic skills, look for ways to broaden your child's repertoire of activities so that he can become more well-rounded. There may be areas in which your child excels, such as art, music, gymnastics, or nature study, but for which there is not sufficient time to explore or enhance during the school year. The summer can be an ideal time to work on these areas of interest.

Ask for specific activities that you will be able to do with your child, keeping in mind that there is a variety of ways that certain skills can be improved. If, for example, your child needs practice retelling the sequence of events in stories that she reads, note that this skill can be practiced equally with television shows and movies that you watch together, as well as books read.

SUMMERTIME LEARNING ACTIVITIES

Summertime fun can lend itself to skills that help with your child's schooling when the summer is over. Here are just a few suggestions:

• Ask children to help with meal or picnic preparation. The kitchen is a great place for learning practical math skills, as you may need to double, triple, or halve the quantities for recipes.

• Shopping is a good arena for learning to deal with money: giving the right amount to a clerk, getting change, and figuring the final prices for items that are anywhere from 10 to 50% off.

• Car trips, either on vacation or around town, lend themselves to using maps. Take a look on a map before you start. Use directional words such as north, east, south, and west, so that children get accustomed to hearing and using this terminology.

• Guide books and travel brochures offer lots of information about the places you visit. Hand the material over to the kids and see what strikes their fancy. In addition to good reading comprehension practice, this is a good way for them to work on their social and negotiating skills.

• Writing comes to the forefront in many ways: keeping a journal of a trip, writing an agenda for a day of activities, sending post cards or letters to friends and family, or labeling items to be kept in a scrapbook are four useful possibilities. The key element to writing is that children understand that it has a purpose.

• Use an atlas for following current events that strike your fancy. News stories can lead to investigating the location of the city or country where they take place. If your family follows the Olympics, use this interest to locate the countries represented in the games being played. If any particular country or sport interests him, use this as a point for jumping off into reading about it.

With the family's intention on keeping skills up, you can have a fun and educational summer.

KINDERGARTEN READINESS

How can you be sure that your child is ready for the first day of kindergarten? If you are conscientious about these guidelines, you have nothing to worry about:

Keep lots of books in your home.

Include fiction and non-fiction. Not all books need to be new; you can get very inexpensive books at library book sales, used book stores, and garage sales. Visit your library once a week and check out the limit. Encourage books as gifts from people who ask what they can give your child for a gift-giving occasion.

Talk to your child.

Explain things. Answer questions and look for answers together when you do not have the answer yourself. When you use descriptive vocabulary, you are giving excellent preparation for words that your child will read in books and hear in other venues.

Provide lots of opportunity for your child to write.

Have a variety of paper and writing tools on hand. Have your child include something if you write to relatives. Manipulation of clay and puzzle pieces help to strengthen little fingers to get them ready for writing. When she writes, stress the formation of lower case letters.

Make your child aware of numbers around her.

Count objects, identify numbers you see, and share your thinking when you figure out problems that use math. Ask your child how he figured out things. Be aware that there are usually many ways to solve math problems — not just one.

Spend time with your child.

There is no substitute for time with your child. He benefits more from time with you than from material possessions you can buy with the money you earn when you are not together.

Limit television, videos and movies that your child sees.

This is a passive activity that also has a negative impact on learning to read. It takes no imagination; your child's sense of imagination is enhanced by reading — not by these sources.

Give your child responsibilities at home.

Jobs help children to feel part of a community, whether that community is a family or a classroom group. Don't worry about perfection; that is less important than the act of doing the work and making the contribution.

Don't give your child everything he wants.

He certainly will not get everything he wants at school! Teachers have too much to do than to have to settle disputes with children who will cut only with the pink scissors or who have to sit in the green chair.

Respect the differences you see among other people.

Our society is rich with people whose language, dress, and food show tremendous variety. Talk about the acceptance of other people and show an interest in their culture.

WHAT THE KINDERGARTEN TEACHER MAY LOOK FOR

Getting ready for school is important. There are ways that you can help your child. A typical kindergarten teacher may expect that when a child enters kindergarten, she would be able to:

- give first name, full name, age, address (house number and street), birthdate (month and day), and phone number

- recognize basic colors

- recognize a large variety of everyday household objects

- pick out the different symbol, object, or letter in a group where several are the same and one is different

- have enough experience with crayons and pencils on paper so that she can copy familiar shapes

- stand or hop on one foot at a time

- count to ten

- point to or touch body parts when asked to identify (hand, arm, elbow, eye, etc.)

- listen to, remember, and follow both one-step directions (Get a blue towel.) and two-step directions (Get a blue towel and put it on the towel bar.)

- name numbers 1 - 5 and match the correct number of objects to them

- write her first name (preferably with only the first letter as a capital letter and all the others lower case)

- show that she is learning to speak understandably and in complete sentences

WHAT THE FIRST GRADE TEACHER MAY LOOK FOR

By the time a child has either completed kindergarten or is entering first grade, most first grade teachers will expect that he is able to:

- give first name, full name, age, address (house number and street), birthdate (month and day), and phone number

- recognize basic colors

- recognize a large variety of everyday household objects

- pick out the different letter or word in a group where several are the same and one is different

- have enough experience with crayons and pencils on paper so that she can copy familiar shapes

- draw a person with at least ten different body parts that he can name

- count to twenty

- recite (not sing) the alphabet

- listen to, remember, and follow both one-step directions (Brush your teeth.) and two-step directions (Brush your teeth and put on your pajamas.)

- name numbers 1 - 10 and match the correct number of objects to them

- recognize all lower case letters when shown, including two versions of letters a and g (a,a, g, g)

- recognize what paired words sound alike (bake-bake) or different (cane-came)

- write first name and last name

- write numbers to seven

MULTIPLE INTELLIGENCES

In Howard Gardner's *Frames of Mind*, he proposes that there are seven main areas in which all people have special skills; he calls them intelligences. His research at Harvard University was in response to the work that Alfred Binet had done in France around 1900. Binet's work led to the formation of an intelligence test; we are all familiar with the "intelligence quotient," or "IQ," the way that intelligence is measured on his test.

This type of IQ test was used as the basis of another one with which most of us are familiar: the Scholastic Aptitude Test (SAT), which is taken my most college-bound high school students.

Both of these tests look predominantly at two types of intelligences: verbal and math. If a person does well on these, s/he is considered "intelligent," and is a candidate for one of the better colleges or universities. But what about everyone else? How many of you who are reading these words have used the phrase "not good at taking tests," when talking either about yourself or your child?

The Multiple Intelligences (MI) theory proposes that there are other measures of intelligence beside these two. I offer this information to you so that you can understand that while many teachers have some knowledge of MI theory, most of our schools are not fully set up to use it to the advantage of all students.

That being the case, perhaps you can either (1) be involved in helping your child's teachers and school to provide a more balanced program that develops his intelligences that are not more included in the curriculum or (2) find activities outside of the school environment in which your child can develop his dominant areas of intelligence.

You should also know that MI theory posits that each of us has, to some degree or another, all of these intelligences. Some of them are simply more developed than others. Furthermore, we are all able to improve our ability in each of these areas.

Because Gardner stresses that the intelligences are equal in their importance, I list the original seven intelligences in alphabetical order:

- Bodily-kinesthetic: using one's body to solve problems and express ideas and feelings. Actors, athletes, and dancers use their whole bodies in this way, much the same way that craftspeople, sculptors, and mechanics use their hands.

- Interpersonal: perceiving the moods, feelings, and needs of others. If you are a "people person," this is a dominant and well-developed intelligence for you. It includes salespeople, teachers, counselors, and those we have come to call the helping professions.

145

- Intrapersonal: turning inward with a well-developed self-knowledge and using it successfully to navigate oneself through the world.

- Linguistic: using words, either orally or written, in an effective manner. This intelligence is associated with storytellers, politicians, comedians, and writers.

- Logical-Mathematical: understanding and using numbers effectively, as well as having good powers to reason well. People who make especially good use of this intelligence are mathemeticians, scientists, computer programmers, and accountants.

- Musical: relating in a wide range of ways to music. This can take many forms; a performer, composer, critic, and music-lover are all making use of this intelligence.

- Spatial: perceiving the visual-spatial world in an accurate way, so as to be able to work in it effectively. The people who do this cover a wide range of fields that, upon first glance, do not seem to have much in common. Compare, for example, hunters, sailors, engineers, inventors, and surgeons to interior decorators, architects, painters, and sculptors.

I have seen limited reference to another intelligence: Naturalist, which is referred to as being able to recognize plant or animal species in the environment. This one is not included in the two Gardner books I list here for your perusal, but was added after this original research.

READ MORE ABOUT MULTIPLE INTELLIGENCES

Howard Gardner's books on this topic are *Frames of Mind* and *Multiple Intelligences: The Theory in Practice*.

In addition, Thomas Armstrong continues the work in his *Multiple Intelligences in the Classroom*. To get a sense of your child's areas of strength, go to www.familyeducation.com, where you can find a page entitled *Test Your Child's Talents*, which is based on Armstrong's book.

NATIONAL SOMETHING-OR-OTHER MONTH

Some of these declarations may have an impact on your child's classroom curriculum, depending on the focus of the teacher or the school. In any event, you may want to use them yourself to stress areas that you think are important to your child.

January

National Eye Care Month

National Book Month

February

National Children's Dental Health Month

Black History Month

Seatbelt Safety Month

March

Irish-American Heritage Month

National Nutrition Month

National Craft Month

National Women's History Month

April

Month of the Young Child

National Keep America Beautiful Month

Math Education Month

National Kite Month

National Humor Month

National Poetry Month

Week of the Young Child

May

National Asian/Pacific Heritage Month

National Older Americans Month

National Physical Fitness and Sports Month

National Teen Pregnancy Prevention Month

National Family Month

National Bike Month

June

American Rivers Month

Zoo & Aquarium Month

National Safety Month

July

National Hot Dog Month

August

National Physically Challenged Month

National Ineventors Month

September

Hispanic Heritage Month, 9/15 - 10/15

October

National UNICEF Month

National Computer Learning Month

November

National American Indian Heritage Month

National Career Development Month